TABLE OF CONTENTS

INTRODUCTION 1

Framing the Thesis 1

Strategic Approach 5

CHAPTER 1: GRAND STRATEGY THEORY 9

Strategic Theory 9

    The Essential Elements of Strategy 9

    Assessing the Effectiveness of Strategy—Validity and Risk 11

Grand Strategy: The Continuation of Policy through Peace and War 12

    The Unbroken Continuum of Grand Strategy 13

    Wisdom and Judgment: The Keys to Effectiveness in Grand Strategy 15

Grand Strategy Theory 18

CHAPTER 2: American Political Theory 21

Colonial American Political Development 23

    The Critical Context of Community 23

    The Foundation for Community: The Core Anglo-Protestant Culture 25

    Covenants, Compacts, Charters, and Constitutions 29

The Political Transformation to the United States of America 35

    The Foundation for Unity: Anglo-American/Protestant Culture 36

    Declaration of Independence 40

    State Constitutions 41

    The Articles of Confederation 42

    The Constitution of the United States 45

American Political Theory 49

    Popular Sovereignty: The Theoretical Balance of Civil Liberty and Order 49

    The Institutional Political Theory of the U.S. Constitution 51

CHAPTER 3: Historical Criticism Of American Grand Strategy 59

America's First and Enduring Grand Strategy 59

    The Ends of American Grand Strategy 61

    The Means of American Grand Strategy 61

    The Ways of American Grand Strategy 65

American Foreign Policy Traditions 67

    America's Foundational Foreign Policy Traditions 68

    Liberty (Exceptionalism) 68

Unilateralism 72

The American System (Monroe Doctrine).. 76

Expansionism 80

The Mexican-American War: A Traditional Punitive War................................. 86

The Civil War: Two Competing Visions of Grand Strategy and Foreign Policy . 94

America's Modern Foreign Policy Traditions..96

The Progressive Movement: A Radical Break from American Tradition 96

Progressive Imperialism.. 102

The Philippine-American War: A War of Progressive Imperialism.................... 110

Wilsonianism (Liberal Internationalism) 113

Containment 118

Global Meliorism 127

The Vietnam War: A War of Global Meliorism 131

Historical Criticism of America's Modern Foreign Policy Traditions 137

Flawed Assumptions and Hidden Risks... 138

Unrealistic Ends and Invalid Strategies 146

CHAPTER 4: American Grand Strategy for the 21st Century 155

Critical Changes in the Strategic Environment 155

Reevaluating American National Identity...156

American Foreign Policy Traditions for the 21st Century 160

Liberty (Exceptionalism) 160

Unilateralism 163

American System/Containment 165

Expansionism 167

CONCLUSION..171

BIBLIOGRAPHY 181

INTRODUCTION

Framing the Thesis

More than a decade after September 11, 2001, the United States is still struggling

to frame a realistic, long-term grand strategy to secure America's vital national interests

in the twenty-first century. After 9/11, the 2002 National Security Strategy viewed the

post-Cold War era through the lens of a new era of liberty: "The great struggles of the

twentieth century between liberty and totalitarianism ended with a decisive victory for the

forces of freedom—and a single sustainable model for national success: freedom,

democracy and free enterprise."[1] The prevailing viewpoint was that the United States

entered the twenty-first century with "unprecedented—and unequaled—strength and

influence in the world," which was to be used to "translate this moment of influence into

decades of peace, prosperity, and liberty."[2] The United States has "spilled American

blood in foreign lands—not to build an empire, but to shape a world in which more

individuals and nations could determine their own destiny, and live with the peace and

dignity that they deserve."[3] This mission continues to endure, though the costs have

begun to take their toll.

Little has changed in the stated strategic ends of America's National Security

Strategy, but much has changed in the strategic environment to challenge the

effectiveness of the strategy used to achieve these ends. After over a decade into this

---

[1] U.S. President, *National Security Strategy* (Washington DC: Government Printing Office, September 2002), 1.

[2] Ibid.

[3] U.S. President, *National Security Strategy* (Washington DC: Government Printing Office, May 2010), 1.

struggle for greater liberty and order in the world, the United States is faced with the harsh reality and costs of two protracted wars, growing international disorder and conflict, as well as, increasingly complex threats in a volatile strategic environment. History will be the final judge, but reality has tempered the idealistic hopes for sustained peaceful democratic governance in Afghanistan and Iraq. America's perspective must also face the reality that the unprecedented and unequaled strength and influence, prevalent after the Cold War, has somewhat waned in a more competitive and complex globalized world due in part to a large and growing national debt and a sustained economic crisis in the wake of two costly protracted wars.

These challenges to the effectiveness of American grand strategy do not diminish the reality of the complex challenges in Afghanistan, Iraq, and the Arab Spring popular uprisings, which highlight the fundamental struggle to *balance liberty and order* within governments and democratic movements. These events also demonstrate the natural tension between governments and their people within nations around the world. Governments will continue to oppress the people and deny them civil liberty in order to maintain civil order. However, America's goal to promote the *balance of liberty and order in foreign nations* has proven far harder to achieve than American political leaders envisioned. This demands a reevaluation of America's own historical political development to reexamine the lessons and challenges of establishing America's constitutional republic.

In the light of the realities in the current strategic environment, American grand strategy must also be reevaluated, which requires answers to some difficult strategic questions. Why is American grand strategy not accomplishing the expected strategic ends? Are these ends realistic? What are the fundamental assumptions? Is there a logical flaw or imbalance in America's grand strategy that has rendered it ineffective or unachievable? If so, where is the problem? Is America's current strategic path in keeping with the historic continuum of American grand strategy? Is it consistent with the enduring principles and traditions that have served as the foundations for the government and foreign policy of the United States? What strategic role is necessary to secure America's vital national interests in the decades to come? Why? These complex questions require a careful analysis of both theory and history.

A contemporary strategic theorist from the Strategic Studies Institute, Harry Yarger, provides a starting point in the search for answers. "Strategy must be integrated into the stream of history; it must be congruous with what has already happened and with *realistic* possibilities of the future."[4] Therefore, this thesis will analyze and examine the continuum of history in order to provide a framework of constants and consistent trends that will likely continue into the future. History does shed light on both the enduring struggle for liberty and order, as well as the continuum of American grand strategy. Analyzing both will assist in understanding the problem and provide insight into developing an effective grand strategy for the 21st century.

American history has much to say about the struggle for liberty and order. This same struggle led the American colonies to proclaim a Declaration of Independence from the tyrannical rule of the British king. The Colonists united to fight for their liberty and the right to govern themselves in the Revolutionary War. However, the Founding Fathers were forced to unite again to replace the Articles of Confederation with the Constitution

---

[4] Harry R. Yarger, "Strategic Theory for the 21st Century: The Little Book on Big Strategy," Strategic Studies Institute (SSI) monograph, Feb 2006, 67, http://www.comw.org/qdr/fulltext/0602yarger.pdf (accessed September 12, 2011).

of the United States, which established a national government strong enough to defend the nation and secure order, while still maintaining civil liberty. This fundamental struggle between liberty and order has not changed because human nature has not changed. Likewise, the fundamental principles that shaped America's foundational documents and established the nation's constitutional republican government are still relevant to this struggle and the balance between liberty and order.

I propose that the same enduring principles of civil liberty and order that framed America's first grand strategy through the Declaration of Independence, the U.S. Constitution and the foreign policy traditions of the Founding Fathers must also frame America's Grand Strategy in the 21st century. In the United States, civil liberty and order is manifested in the consensual symbiotic relationship between the *people*, *communities* and the *government*. Together, the Declaration of Independence and the Constitution of the United States codified the foundation of America's first grand strategy to establish and sustain civil liberty and order in the United States. The Founding Fathers established these founding documents and foreign policy traditions to define America's strategic political *ends,* and provide the *ways* and the *means* to achieve those *ends*. The Constitution defines vital national *interests* and strategic *ends*, and the institutional mechanisms to provide the strategic *means*. The foreign policy traditions further clarify *ends*, and specify strategic *ways* and *means* to promote and secure national interests in the strategic environment.

Strategic Approach

The strategic approach used to develop this thesis follows Carl von Clausewitz's approach to "critical analysis" in his classic volume, *On War*.[5] Clausewitz described the critic's task as "investigating the relation of cause and effect and the appropriateness of means to ends."[6] This critical approach contains three key elements: historical research, critical analysis, and criticism. Historical research is the discovery of historical facts. Critical analysis is the "tracing of effects back to their causes."[7] Taken together, the historic compilation of cause and effect forms the basis to create a working theory. The last step is criticism, which constitutes the "investigation and evaluation of the means employed."[8] A working theory is essential to conduct a useful criticism. Clausewitz warned "Without such a theory it is generally impossible for criticism to reach that point at which it becomes truly instructive" because theory is the mechanism that illuminates history.[9] Ultimately, criticism reveals the "lessons to be drawn from history"—not as "laws or standards, but only…as aids to *judgment*" in order to gain *wisdom* to shape future strategy.[10]

The thesis will be developed using this critical analysis approach. The first chapter explores the theoretical fundamentals of strategy to understand the essential elements and nature of grand strategy and the critical role it plays in the continuum of history through both war and peace. The second chapter surveys and analyzes the

---

[5] Carl Von Clausewitz, *On War*, ed. and trans. Michael Howard and Peter Paret (Oxford: New York: Alfred A. Knopf, Inc., 1993), 181.

[6] Ibid.

[7] Ibid.

[8] Ibid.

[9] Ibid., 183.

[10] Ibid., 181-183.

historical development of American self-government in order to develop the fundamental principles of political theory that serve as the foundation of the Declaration of Independence and the Constitution of the United States. The third chapter is the heart of the critical analysis. The historical continuum of American grand strategy since 1776 will be systematically criticized through the lens of grand strategy and American political theory. The purpose of this criticism is to evaluate the effectiveness of the means utilized by America's grand strategy in the continuum of history to maintain the balance between civil liberty and order.

The theory of strategy, particularly grand strategy, will be developed first as the *logical* framework to evaluate the continuum of American grand strategy. Strategy is designed to achieve specified *ends* by utilizing *ways* and *means* specifically designed to maximize *effectiveness* but minimize *risk* in the *strategic environment*.[11] Grand strategy represents strategy at the national level to promote and secure national *interests* in the continuum of both peace and war. As part of grand strategy, foreign and domestic *policies* codify national *interests* as *ends*, along with *ways* and *means* judged most *effective* in the *strategic environment* with the least amount of *risk*.[12] In order to minimize *risk*, the *logic* of strategy must remain *valid*. Therefore, strategy must be based on a solid foundation of realistic *assumptions* and a consistent logical construct that maintains the balanced equilibrium between *ends*, *ways* and *means* to ensure the *suitability, acceptability,* and *feasibility*. This understanding of the theoretical elements of grand strategy will provide the framework for a historical analysis and criticism of the continuum of American grand strategy.

---

[11] Yarger, 65.

[12] Ibid., 5.

Next, a historical analysis of American political development will be conducted in order to develop a working American political theory to evaluate the means utilized to balance and sustain liberty and order. This will also foster a deeper understanding of the American political theory that serves as the model to shape the world. The increasingly complex forms of self-government in the American Colonies from 1620 to 1787 will be surveyed using the comprehensive analysis of Donald Lutz, as well as original documents and writings of the period, such as *The Federalist Papers*.[13] The chapter will specifically analyze the community-centric political development that resulted in a sophisticated American political theory based on *popular sovereignty*, which fundamentally shaped the Declaration of Independence and the U.S. Constitution. *Popular sovereignty* is the political idea that the *community* and its *government* originate in the *consent* of the *people*. *Popular sovereignty* created and sustained *civil liberty* through the symbiotic consensual relationship created between the people, the community, and the government, which balanced individual freedom with obedience, and civil rights with civil responsibilities. *Civil liberty* represented the balance *between liberty and order* that resulted from this symbiotic consensual relationship. Therefore, in America, *popular sovereignty* represented the foundational means of sustaining *civil liberty*—the *balance between liberty and order*. The Founding Fathers combined popular sovereignty with institutional design concepts to form the political theory that framed the Constitution. This political theory will form the basis of criticism to evaluate the continuum of American grand strategy.

---

[13] Lutz has meticulously researched the original manuscripts, political writings and theories of the period for more than 25 years, which culminated in his fourth book on the subject, *The Origins of Constitutionalism*. Thomas Jefferson endorsed *The Federalist Papers* as "an authority…as evidence of the general opinion of those who framed, and of those who accepted the Constitution of the United States, on questions as to its genuine meaning."

The historical criticism of American grand strategy will be evaluated using the founding documents and the major foreign policy traditions that were developed from 1776 to the present wars in Afghanistan and Iraq. Walter McDougall, a Pulitzer Prize winning historian, has categorized eight major American foreign policy traditions during this period, which will serve as the baseline for the critical analysis. The first four—Liberty/Exceptionalism, Unilateralism, the American System, and Expansionism—were developed by the Founding Fathers. These traditions dominated foreign policy until 1898. However, four more modern foreign policy traditions have vied for dominance in the 20th and 21st centuries—Progressive Imperialism, Wilsonianism, Containment, and Global Meliorism.[14] The critical analysis and historical criticism of these eight foreign policy traditions highlight the *effectiveness* of each of these foreign policy traditions in achieving America's strategic ends.

The historical criticism and the lessons learned from this criticism will be used to make recommendations to reframe American grand strategy for the 21st century. Reframing American foreign policy on the solid foundation established by the Founding Fathers in the U.S. Constitution and their foreign policy traditions will minimize the strategic *risk* to America's vital national interests. This will also restore the *effectiveness* of American grand strategy in the 21st century strategic environment.

---

[14] Walter A. McDougall, *Promised Land, Crusader State: The American Encounter with the World Since 1776* (New York: Houghton Mifflin Company, 1997), 10-11.

CHAPTER 1: GRAND STRATEGY THEORY

Strategic Theory

Strategic theory forms the foundation for the analysis of American grand strategy. Harry Yarger developed a comprehensive strategic theory in his foundational monograph, "Strategic Theory for the 21st Century: The Little Book on Big Strategy," which consolidated the thinking of many of the greatest strategic theorists such as Carl von Clausewitz, Arthur Lykke, Jr., Colin Gray and others. As a starting point, strategy defines "*how* (concept or *way*) leadership will use the *power* (resources or *means*) available to the state to exercise control over sets of circumstances and geographic locations [strategic environment] to achieve *objectives* (*ends*) in accordance with state *policy*."[1]

The Essential Elements of Strategy

Theoretically, strategy is "a method of creating strategic effects favorable to *policy* and *interests* by applying *ends, ways* and *means* in the *strategic environment*."[2] *Interests* are simply "desired end states" that the nation-state naturally and consistently pursues, and *policy* is the "expression of the desired end state."[3] Together, e*nds, ways* and *means* form the *logical construct* of strategy to achieve those end states. *Ends* "explain 'what' is to be accomplished;" w*ays* "answer the big questions of 'how' the objectives are to be accomplished" and link ends to means by "addressing who does

---

[1] Harry R. Yarger, "Strategic Theory for the 21st Century: The Little Book on Big Strategy," Strategic Studies Institute (SSI) monograph, Feb 2006, 6, http://www.comw.org/qdr/fulltext/0602yarger.pdf (accessed September 12, 2011).

[2] Ibid., 5-7.

[3] Ibid.

what, where, when, how, and why"; and m*eans* answer the question "with what" and are defined by quantifiable resources or power to pursue the ways.[4] The internal and external *strategic environment* respectively covers both the domestic and foreign environment, which provides the context for national *interests*, as well as, domestic and foreign *policy*.[5] The strategic environment is characterized by "volatility, uncertainty, complexity, and ambiguity (VUCA)."[6] Strategy must account for the human element of the strategic environment, which independently acts, reacts and interacts dynamically. Clausewitz characterized these dynamics as fog, friction and chance, which demand that strategy "must be *flexible* and *adaptable*" to effectively react to the "unforeseen."[7] Therefore, strategy must incorporate *flexibility* and *adaptability* to maintain effectiveness in the VUCA strategic environment.

The following working model of strategic theory frames the complex interrelationships between the critical elements of strategy developed throughout this analysis. Strategy is the art and science of designing a *suitable, acceptable,* and *feasible* combination of balanced *ends, ways* and *means* that maximize *effectiveness* in achieving *policy* goals and objectives by favorably affecting or mitigating the foreign and domestic *strategic environment* with sufficient *flexibility* and *adaptability* to minimize *risk* to *interests*.

---

[4] Ibid., 69.

[5] Ibid., 7.

[6] Ibid., 18.

[7] Ibid., 53.

Assessing the Effectiveness of Strategy—Validity and Risk

Strategy requires a logical balance to be effective because if the ends, ways, and means are not balanced the strategy is not logically *valid*. According to Yarger, the logical validity of the strategy is determined through three tests—"suitability, acceptability, and feasibility"—in order to ensure "a synergistic balance of ends, ways, and means."[8]

- Suitability: Can the strategic *end* be achieved in the strategic environment using the selected *ways* and *means*?

- Feasibility: Are the *means* available sufficient to execute the *ways* selected? Can sufficient *means* be sustained long enough to achieve the strategic *end*?

- Acceptability: Are the selected *ways* and *means* in accordance with American values? Do the *ends* justify the *means* to the American public? Are the selected ways and means acceptable to the government and/or the people of the affected foreign nation(s)?

In essence, these questions test for logical imbalances or disconnects between the ends, ways and means of the strategy. If they are not in balance, then the strategy is not logically *valid*.

Risk is a much more complex and subjective assessment utilizing a comprehensive cost/benefit analysis of the strategy in the context of the strategic environment. The goal of an *effective* strategy is to minimize *risk* and maximize the benefits in the resulting interaction with the strategic environment. However, the difficulty lies in accurately assessing the VUCA nature of the strategic environment, which relies almost entirely on a realistic "balance among what is known, *assumed*, and unknown."[9] Just as in a logical argument, unrealistic *assumptions* will lead to false

---

[8] Ibid., 68, 70.
[9] Ibid., 63.

11

conclusions and an unrealistic assessment of *risk*. Unfortunately, an unrealistic risk assessment usually results in real and sometimes catastrophic consequences.

Risk must also take into account both the "probability of success *or* failure," as well as, "the probable consequences of success *and* failure."[10] Risk measures the probability of achieving success without creating "unintended adverse effects of such magnitude as to negate what would otherwise be regarded as strategic success."[11] However, risk also must account for the *consequences* of the strategy whether it is successful or not. As an example, in foreign policy, a risk assessment must weigh the *benefits* of achieving success towards a stated strategic end to promote international order versus the probable domestic *consequences,* such as "costs in blood, treasure and potential insecurity" at home to achieve that success.[12] Ultimately, the risk assessment should assist political leaders and commanders in assessing whether the strategy is effective in order to determine whether the strategy should be "accepted, modified or rejected."[13]

Grand Strategy: The Continuation of Policy through Peace and War

Grand strategy involves a much broader perspective as a comprehensive national strategy designed to promote and secure *national interests* in the continuation of *national policy* through war and peace. The definitions of interests and policy take on a much broader national perspective in grand strategy. *National interests* are simply national goals or end states for the good of the country and the people. The Founding Fathers

---

[10] Ibid., 63.

[11] Ibid., 68.

[12] Ibid., 70.

[13] Ibid., 64.

defined the enduring, *vital* national interests of the United States in the Preamble of the Constitution. National leaders must exercise great *"wisdom* and *judgment"[14]* to promote and secure these vital *national interests* through the ends, ways and means of *grand strategy* with the requisite *flexibility* and *adaptability* to sustain effectiveness in the VUCA strategic environment.

The Unbroken Continuum of Grand Strategy

Grand strategy defines the strategic ends, ways and means in national policy to promote and secure national interests in both war and peace. Carl Von Clausewitz, in his classic *On War*, states: "War is merely the continuation of policy by other means…a true political instrument, a continuation of political intercourse."[15] Thus, political leaders define the political ends via *national policy* and war strategy defines the *ways* and *means* in which the political *ends* are achieved. However, Clausewitz also describes *policy* as a broader political strategy that utilizes means other than war in the continuation of political intercourse. Therefore, national policy must account for the specific context of the strategic environment and the impacts to national interests.   In theory, "policy is the clear articulation of guidance for the employment of the instruments of power towards the attainment of one or more objectives [ends] or end states."[16] However, this guidance is best articulated through the logic of strategy in order to determine the most *effective* way to secure national interests in the strategic environment with minimum *risk*. Therefore, national policy and grand strategy are linked through an ongoing iterative

---

[14] Paul Kennedy, *Grand Strategies in War and Peace* (New Haven: Yale University Press, 1991), 6.

[15] Carl Von Clausewitz, *On War*, ed. and trans. Michael Howard and PeterParet (Oxford: New York: Alfred A. Knopf, Inc., 1993), 99.

[16] Yarger, 7.

process. "The development of strategy informs policy; policy must adapt itself to the realities of the strategic environment and the limits of power. Thus policy ensures that strategy pursues appropriate aims, while strategy informs policy of the art of the possible."[17] Grand strategy and national policy are two sides of the same coin, closely interrelated and inseparable. Paul Kennedy describes policy as "the crux of grand strategy," because it harnesses "all of the elements, both military and non-military, for the preservation and enhancement of the nation's long-term (that is, in wartime and peacetime) best interests."[18] The great British strategist B. H. Liddell Hart also defines this broader political level of strategy as "grand strategy."[19] Therefore, grand strategy defines the ends, ways and means required to promote and secure the national interests in the broader continuation of policy through both peace and war.

Grand strategy must also operate effectively in both peace and war across the unbroken continuum of history. Paul Kennedy confirms this continuum, since "true grand strategy was now concerned with peace as much as (perhaps even more than) with war" concerning the "evolution and integration of policies that should operate for decades, or even for centuries."[20] Grand strategy should remain consistent over time, while preserving the flexibility and adaptability to protect the long-term, vital national interests in the context of the changing realities of the strategic environment. Therefore, in grand strategy, the development of ends, ways and means must be balanced in order to remain valid and effective in both war and peace.

---

[17] Ibid., 7, 51.

[18] Kennedy, 5.

[19] B. H. Liddell Hart, *Strategy* (New York: Penguin Group, 1991), 321.

[20] Kennedy, 4.

Wisdom and Judgment: The Keys to Effectiveness in Grand Strategy

In grand strategy, political leaders must exercise wisdom and judgment to ensure that strategic *ends* are *realistic* in order to mitigate risk and be truly *effective* in promoting and securing national interests. Wisdom and judgment are required to develop realistic strategic ends to mitigate the challenges of the strategic environment in order to promote and secure national interests. The wisdom and judgment of leaders should be "formed, and refined, by experience—including the study of historical experiences."[21] A common theme through history is the "demand placed upon the *polities* of this world, whether ancient empires or modern democracies, to devise ways of enabling them to survive and flourish in an anarchic and often threatening international order that oscillates between peace and war, and is always changing."[22] Unfortunately, idealistic political leaders sometimes unknowingly introduce strategic *risk* to the nation's *vital* national interests through overly ambitious or *unrealistic strategic ends* based on a *false assumption*. Therefore, grand strategy may be rendered ineffective because of the hidden *risk* introduced by the false assumption. In this case, the true nature and magnitude of the risk will not be exposed until the strategy is implemented and interacts negatively with the harsh reality of the strategic environment. However, the consequences are much higher in grand strategy, since risks are likely to impact a nation's *vital* national interests, which could threaten a nation's survival or way of life. History testifies repeatedly that the consequences of assuming too much risk in grand strategy usually exacts a terrible cost on a nation. It is critical to examine all assumptions within grand strategy to ensure the *ends* of grand strategy reflect the *reality* of the strategic environment.

---

[21] Ibid., 6.

[22] Ibid.

Wisdom and judgment are also required to develop and resource the broader set of *means* required for the continuation of policy in grand strategy. Since grand strategy governs the unbroken continuum of national policy through both peace and war, the choices of *means* must be expanded beyond war and military *means* to be effective in promoting and securing long-term vital national interests. Liddell Hart describes a broader set of political instruments more suitable for grand strategy. The military or "fighting power is but one of the instruments of grand strategy—which should take account of and apply the power of financial pressure, of diplomatic pressure, of commercial pressure, and not the least of ethical pressure, to weaken the opponent's will."[23] Though Liddell Hart refers to them as various pressures, these correspond to what is more commonly known today in doctrine as the instruments of national power— Diplomatic, Informational, Military and Economic or DIME.[24] These additional instruments of national power outside of the military open up the range of options that national leaders can select to promote and secure national interests whether the context is war or peace.

Political leaders must also exercise wisdom and judgment to maintain the logical balance between *ends* and *means* to ensure grand strategy remains *suitable*, *acceptable* and *feasible* to achieve long-term success and victory. Liddell Hart applies the long view of history to the subject of true victory in grand strategy: "Victory in the true sense implies that the state of peace, and of one's people, is better after the war than before."[25] Grand strategy must be *suitable* to achieve strategic *ends* without jeopardizing the vital

---

[23] Hart, 321-22.

[24] Yarger, 5.

[25] Hart, 357.

national interests and the state of the people. However, the *ends* do not justify any *means* available. True victory also requires that grand strategy remain *acceptable* to the people—and in most cases, the international community—so that the state of peace is not compromised. Hart further explains the requirements for true victory. "Victory in this sense is only possible if a quick result can be gained or if a long effort can be economically proportioned to the national resources. The *end* must be adjusted to the *means*."[26] Therefore, sufficient means must be sustained to achieve desired strategic ends. Otherwise, if the means are insufficient or unsustainable to achieve the strategic end, then the strategy is not *feasible* and vital national interests are vulnerable. The consequences of insufficient means is that the nation will rarely achieve true victory and risks overall strategic failure. True success or victory is directly linked to how well a nation's grand strategy maintains the long-term balance of *ends* versus *means* to sustain a long-term *valid* strategy through both war and peace.

A nation's political leaders require wisdom and judgment to sufficiently resource and maintain a *balanced portfolio* of means—the instruments of power (DIME)—to sustain *flexibility* and *adaptability* in grand strategy in order to mitigate *risk*. Flexibility and adaptability are "relative to the ability of the state to bring to bear the whole range of the capabilities inherent to its elements of power," which enables grand strategy to remain effective despite the dynamic "realities of the strategic environment and the limits of power."[27] The bottom line is that the power of a nation is driven by *means*, and *means* are always restricted by limited resources. Since the nation is faced with limited resources, national interests must be prioritized to determine *vital* national interests, so

---

[26] Ibid.

[27] Yarger, 7, 59.

that the quantity and variety of instruments of power can be prioritized and resourced accordingly. Grand strategy must "calculate and develop" all of the various instruments of power sufficiently to provide for national "security and prosperity."[28] Disregarding this wise counsel degrades the effectiveness of a nation's grand strategy and introduces significant risk. For example, if a strong military is maintained at the cost of other instruments of power, then the nation is limited to the "military hammer" and all threats begin to look like nails, regardless of the realities of the strategic environment.[29] A broad diversification of power mitigates risk.[30] Political leaders require wisdom and judgment to maintain a balanced portfolio of means (DIME) to ensure sufficient *flexibility* and *adaptability* in order to sustain strategic effectiveness in both peace and war.

Grand Strategy Theory

In light of this theoretical discussion, the following working model of grand strategy will be used to conduct this critical analysis. Grand strategy is the art and science of designing a suitable, acceptable, and feasible combination of balanced ends, ways and means in order to maximize effectiveness *in promoting and securing national interests* by favorably affecting or mitigating the foreign and domestic strategic environment with sufficient flexibility and adaptability to minimize risk to the *vital* national interests throughout *the broad continuum of peace and war*.

Political leaders require *wisdom* and *judgment* to design a *valid* and sustainable grand strategy that effectively promotes and secures *national interests* while mitigating *risk* to *vital* national interests in both war and peace. A sustainable balance must always

---

[28] Hart, 322.

[29] Yarger, 59.

[30] Ibid.

be maintained in a nation's grand strategy because the consequences of the risk may jeopardize the nation's survival or way of life. Grand strategy, by its very nature, must have a long-term perspective with a focus on the mitigation of risk because of the severity of the strategic consequences. Ultimately, political leaders must exercise wisdom and judgment to: 1) develop *realistic ends* that avoid *idealistic assumptions* about the strategic environment; 2) resource a *broad portfolio of means*—the DIME instruments of power—to remain effective across the broad continuum of war and peace; 3) maintain a long-term *balance* between *ends* and *means* to ensure that the grand strategy remains *valid—suitable, acceptable,* and *feasible*; and 4) sustain a *balanced portfolio of means* to maintain the *flexibility* and *adaptability* to ensure continued effectiveness in a VUCA strategic environment. This sort of wisdom and judgment can only be achieved through the study of historical experiences, which is further forged and tested through practical experience.

This theoretical understanding of grand strategy provides the framework to evaluate the historical continuum of American grand strategy. However, before American grand strategy can be analyzed, the foundations of this nation's grand strategy must be understood. The historical political developments of America forged the fundamental principles of civil liberty. These fundamental principles and the founding documents that enshrined them form the foundation of American grand strategy. They were developed through the wisdom and judgment of the Founding Fathers, who were steeped in history and guided by collective practical experience. This solid foundation is the reason these founding principles and documents remain essential and relevant to American grand strategy today.

CHAPTER 2: AMERICAN POLITICAL THEORY

In the United States, grand strategy and political theory are intertwined because the Constitution is the foundation of both the American government and grand strategy. Americans tend to take their political freedoms and heritage for granted. Few understand the innovative constitutional institutions that protect their civil liberty and maintain civil order. Fewer still truly understand how the greatest nation on earth developed from small isolated pockets of British colonists. America's transformation from these small colonial communities to a unified constitutional republic must be carefully analyzed to understand the gradual political development and unique conditions within America that forged the Constitution of the United States, particularly if the American model is to be exported.

Colonial America benefited from ideal conditions for political development because of a common culture and a common political preference for representative government that served as the foundation to unify the people into a *constitutional republic* with a strong national identity. Each of the thirteen original colonies started as small isolated communities with representative municipal governments that united together in larger combined communities, which required more complex federated governments. In 1776, these relatively homogeneous colonies united as *a people*—united in common purpose and "bound together by widely held values, interests, and goals" based on their common Anglo-American/Protestant culture—in the Declaration of Independence.[1] The development of the State Constitutions and the U.S. Constitution completed the transformation to a great republic—the United States of America.

---

[1] Donald S. Lutz, *The Origins of American Constitutionalism* (Baton Rouge: Louisiana State University Press, 1988), 6.

The founding documents—the Declaration of Independence, the State Constitutions and the U.S. Constitution—defined the United States and represented the culmination of over a century and a half of American political development. "In 1787, the only written constitutions in the world existed in English-speaking America."[2] At the time of the Constitutional Convention, the Founding Fathers already had practical experience writing and executing "two dozen state constitutions and the national Articles of Confederation."[3] The practical wisdom and judgment of the Founding Fathers was critical to the innovative strategic design of the Constitution. The U.S. Constitution became the quintessential "document of political founding." As a constitution in the unique tradition of American constitutionalism, it codified all institutional "political commitments" and became the standard by which Americans "assess, develop and run our political system."[4] The Constitution and the State Constitutions defined an integrated and symbiotic political system that established the innovative republican national government, which governed the United States in conjunction with the corresponding state and municipal governments.

The Declaration of Independence and the Constitution also served as America's first and enduring grand strategy, which mitigated the risks associated with human nature in both the domestic and foreign strategic environment. These documents codified the institutional principles of popular sovereignty, which established the foundation of civil liberty and order in America. Understanding the domestic political grand strategy of the

---

[2] Ibid.

[3] Ibid., 5.

[4] Ibid., 3.

Founding Fathers in the Constitution is essential to understanding the historical continuum of foreign policy in American grand strategy.

Colonial American Political Development

In the American colonies, each community was established by the individual consent of the people who freely decided to unite themselves as a community. These established communities served as the foundation for all other political development in America. Representative municipal governments were formed based on the consent of the people. These governments became more complex as communities grew and combined. Various political documents defined these communities and their institutional form of government, which included covenants, compacts, charters, and eventually constitutions.

The Critical Context of Community

America developed as a "nation of communities," so political development can only be understood in the context of community.[5] These communities were formed by the consent of the people, resulting from the common Anglo-Protestant culture of the settlers. These communities developed at the local level where people met together, face to face, and consented to unite themselves and their families for mutual benefit. This was a personal decision and the people signed their names on the document designed to establish the community. In America, it was *communities*, not individuals, which united and combined to create *a people*.[6]

---

[5] Ibid., 71.

[6] Ibid.

Communities in America were formed by the *consent* of the people, and consent was only possible because each individual had the *liberty* to choose. Individual *consent* is foundational because it forms the basis for the communitarian context of American political development. Community membership required mutual and unanimous consent, because an "agreement creating a people should be unanimous, for those not agreeing are not bound by it."[7] Community membership required unanimous agreement, because consent *bound* the individual to the governance of the community, which was governed by majority rule. Consent to join the community was consent to submit to the majority rule of the community.[8] Therefore, *consent* was the foundation of *civil order* in America. However, without *liberty* there can be no *consent*. This combination of liberty and consent formed the conceptual foundation of American civil liberty.

Civil Liberty was a much more complex concept in colonial America than simple liberty or freedom. Individual freedom was defined as *natural liberty*. *Natural liberty* represented the state of man, as an accountable creature, in which "everyone is free to act as he thinks fit," subject to the same "Laws of Nature and Nature's God" invoked in the Declaration of Independence.[9] However, *civil liberty* further restricted natural liberty in the context of community. "*Civil liberty* is natural liberty restricted by established laws as is expedient or necessary for the good of the community."[10] Each individual had the natural liberty to choose to be a member of a community, but membership required the sacrifice of some of their natural liberty to enjoy the benefits of community in colonial

---

[7] Ibid., 152.

[8] Ibid., 81.

[9] Ibid., 73.

[10] Ibid.

America. Liberty in the American context—the context of community—is *civil liberty* because it represented liberty restricted by the consensual responsibility to obey the laws of the community established by majority rule in order to sustain civil order. Civil liberty represented a balance between freedom and obedience; civil rights and civil responsibilities; liberty and order. Therefore, in America, the *community* established the foundation of the *balance between liberty and order—civil liberty*—through consent and majority rule.

Communities were based on "commonly held set of *values, interests, and rights*" of the people within the community.[11] Carving a colonial foothold in the American wilderness posed a constant threat to the colonists since they lived on the "edge of extinction."[12] Thus, there was a common *interest* in seeking the benefits and protection of a community working together for the common good. "Far from valuing complete independence in a virtual state of nature, Americans above all valued the communities in which they lived."[13] *Interests* for protection and prosperity were powerful motivators to form and consolidate communities. However, these factors alone do not explain the broad-based consent to membership or the long-term stability and growth of these communities. The common culture of the colonists proved to be a powerful factor that drove widespread consent to form, and consolidate, communities in colonial America.

The Foundation for Community: The Core Anglo-Protestant Culture

The predominant Anglo-Protestant values and beliefs prevalent in colonial America enabled community consent and civil liberty. In his "monumental study" of

---

[11] Ibid., 73.

[12] Ibid., 29.

[13] Ibid., 71.

seventeenth century British settlers, David Hacket Fischer discovered a "common culture" in four distinct groups of settlers despite differences in origin, "socioeconomic status" and "specific religious affiliations" because "Virtually all of them…spoke English, were Protestants, adhered to British legal tradition, and valued British liberties."[14] This common Anglo-Protestant culture and Judeo-Christian beliefs made the developing American communities relatively uniform across the colonies.[15] Anglo-Protestant culture brought several dominant beliefs to the New World that shaped America's colonial core *values* and civil *rights*.[16] American Protestantism was born out of the European Protestant Reformation. However, it was a more dissident version, characterized by a "fierce spirit of liberty" that emphasized the individual's responsibility to "learn God's truths directly from the Bible" versus the prevailing "fear, awe, duty, and reverence Englishmen felt toward political and religious authority."[17] Protestantism promoted liberty, equality, and the fundamental rights of freedom of religion and speech, but also stressed a hard work ethic with personal responsibility for success or failure. Individuals and families consented to join communities because of a common culture consisting of the same core beliefs about *values* and *rights,* which created stable and relatively uniform communities throughout the colonies. The power of consent to unite people into communities springs largely from this common core culture because it has the power to overcome inevitable human differences through common beliefs about *values* and *rights*.

---

[14] Samuel P. Huntington, *Who Are We? The Challenges to America's National Identity* (New York: Simon & Schuster Paperbacks, 2005), 42.

[15] Ibid., 64.

[16] Ibid., 62.

[17] Ibid., 63, 68.

Despite a homogeneous religious culture and a common set of core values and rights, self-government was still required to govern these communities in order to maintain civil order and protect civil liberty. In order for self-government to work, the people must collectively have *virtue*, or the "inclination to pursue the common good."[18] "Human nature being what it is, the colonies did not lack people who sought other than the common good."[19] In colonial times, to "follow self-interest or the interest of the minority was the essence of corruption."[20] This posed one of the biggest challenges to these consent-based communities. In essence, the solution required a form of government that exhibited sufficient collective *virtue* in the majority rule to ensure decisions and laws were based on the good of the community, and effectively mediated inevitable conflicts between the majority and self-interested minority factions. A balance had to be maintained between protecting individual civil rights—civil liberty—and securing the good of the community—civil order.

The Anglo-Protestant culture also played a major role in shaping the form of self-government selected to promote and secure the common interests of the community, protect civil liberty and maintain civil order. Protestants historically relied on "congregational forms of church organization," which caused them to favor representative "democratic forms" of government to govern the colonies over more authoritarian forms.[21] The colonists used similar congregational forms of government that "centered on a representative assembly beholden to a virtuous people" in order to

---

[18] Lutz, 29.

[19] Ibid., 17.

[20] Ibid., 29.

[21] Huntington, *Who Are We?*, 68.

27

establish a "deliberative process" to govern the community by majority rule based on the consent of the people.[22] The political logic of this form of self-government was that since the "majority speaks for the community" and the majority elects the legislature, the legislature "represents the community."[23] Representative legislatures were created via majority rule to establish the rule of law to protect civil liberty and ensure civil order. These self-governments still relied heavily on consensus building to maintain civil order, since "survival and/or prosperity demanded that the community move relatively free of *faction*, and repression was rejected as the means of achieving cooperative behavior."[24] However, if an individual refused to obey the majority decision or the rule of law, then he was subject to punishment or even banishment from the community to enforce civil order.

This relatively weak form of representative self-government worked for the colonists due to the common core culture and relative uniformity of consent. This form of self-government was prevalent throughout the colonies. Therefore, the "strong communitarian basis" of the colonial religious values was instrumental in establishing a common colonial framework for representative self-government, which served as the foundational model to protect civil liberty and maintain civil order in the largely consensual environment of colonial communities.[25] This cultural community foundation is clearly demonstrated in the covenants, compacts, and prototypical constitutions

---

[22] Lutz, 27.

[23] Ibid., 95.

[24] Ibid., 29.

[25] Ibid.

developed by the colonists to define their communities and codify their government institutions.

Covenants, Compacts, Charters, and Constitutions

The early settlements of the Puritans and Pilgrims shaped colonial America with their strong Anglo-Protestant culture and beliefs, as well as the representative self-governments they developed.[26] Samuel Huntington calls the Puritans and Pilgrims the "charter group" of the American colonies because they shaped the core values, interests, and rights of the developing communities and founded a settler society in the New World.[27] These "charter groups" formally established "settler societies" by legally defining their communities with *charters,* and *compacts* with the influence of their church *covenants*.[28] The 1620 Mayflower Compact is representative of a charter group compact that established one of the first Puritan settler communities based on biblical precepts to secure cooperation of the settlers for the common good of the community. This and other covenants, compacts and charters provided the foundation for American political development across the colonies that led to the Constitution of the United States.

The North American British colonies were launched under the full legal authorization and control of British charters. A charter was a "sovereign's unilateral grant," which established the power and authority of the sovereign or government over the people in the political relationship.[29] Early colonial charters required pledges of loyalty to the British Crown. However, due to the remoteness of the colonies, local

---

[26] Huntington, *Who Are We?*, 40, 64-65.

[27] Ibid., 64-65.

[28] Ibid., 43.

[29] Lutz, 151.

governance was granted to the colonists within the confines of English common law, albeit under the "nominal control of a board of directors in London."[30] Without the tangible support of an established local government, the new colonies organized themselves into communities to ensure cooperation from each settler in order to survive. Therefore, local self-government formed quickly in the colonies out of necessity.[31]

Legally, the colonists created "legislatures, not governments" through covenants and compacts to establish legitimate forms of community self-government. This was a central feature in colonial self-government. "The legislature represented the community to the Crown and protected the people from the government. It was not part of the government itself."[32] Covenants and compacts represented an agreement between the people themselves to unite for a purpose. A compact formalized an agreement based on the *consent* of the people to create a community.[33] However, a covenant was legally binding because "the highest authority"—either the British Crown or God—witnessed it as a legal document.[34]

Covenants were central to the development of colonial self-government. Church covenants served as a template for local political covenants. The early Protestant colonists in the late 1500's and early 1600's were familiar and comfortable with using "religious covenants as the basis to form communities," so one of the first priorities for colonies was to "covenant a church among themselves."[35] The covenant was secured and

---

[30] Ibid., 24.

[31] Ibid.

[32] Ibid., 152.

[33] Ibid., 17.

[34] Ibid.

[35] Ibid., 7, 24-25.

witnessed by God in accordance with the biblical covenant tradition in the Old

Testament—God's covenant with the "tribes of Israel" to establish them as "a nation."[36]

Besides the witness, the covenant form contains four elements: 1) why the agreement is

necessary; 2) the creation of a people; 3) the creation of an institution (church,

government, etc.); and 4) what they wish to become as a people.[37]

The Puritans developed the Mayflower Compact in 1620 using this same

covenant form and fundamental elements to establish a local government—a "civil Body

Politick"—in accordance with their charter, which was typical of the political covenants

of the time. It represents both a compact and a covenant with all of the four essential

elements.

> In the Name of God, Amen. We whose names are under-written, the
> Loyal Subjects of…King James…Having undertaken for the Glory of
> God, and Advancement of the Christian Faith, and the honor of our King
> and Country, a Voyage to plant the first Colony in the first part northern
> Parts of Virginia; Do by these Presents, solemnly and mutually, in the
> presence of God and one another, covenant and combine ourselves
> together into a civil Body Politick, for our better Ordering and
> Preservation, and Furtherance of the ends aforesaid: And by Virtue hereof
> do enact, constitute, and frame, such just and equal Laws, Ordinances,
> Acts, Constitutions, and Officers, from time to time, as shall be thought
> most meet and convenient for the general Good of the Colony; unto which
> we promise all Submission and Obedience.[38]

Compacts were also prominent in the early colonial political development as

covenants were secularized and the people themselves replaced God as the witness and

---

[36] Ibid., 24-25, 43.

[37] Ibid., 25.

[38] Mayflower Compact. "Mayflower Compact: Agreement Between the Settlers at New Plymouth, 1620." Avalon Project: Documents in Law, History and Diplomacy. Lillian Goldman Law Library, Yale Law School. http://avalon.law.yale.edu/17th_century/mayflower.asp (accessed September 12, 2011).

the authority that secured the covenant.[39] The distinction between a covenant and

compact seems small, but it is a significant distinction in American political

development. The implication of a compact is that the people themselves provide the

sovereign power to enforce the agreement. This marks the beginning of the political

concept of *popular sovereignty* in America —"the idea that the community and its

government originate in the consent of the people."[40]

The "first explicit use of popular sovereignty in America" is contained in the

Providence (Rhode Island) Agreement of 1637.

> We whose names are hereunder, desirous to inhabit in the town of
> Providence, do promise to subject ourselves in active and passive
> obedience to all such orders and agreements as shall be made for the
> public good of the body in an orderly way, by the major consent of present
> inhabitants, masters of families, incorporated together in a Towne
> fellowship, and others whom they shall admit unto them only in civil
> things.[41]

Ironically, the "Towne fellowship" referred to in this secularized agreement is based on a

church fellowship. However, this agreement explicitly extends the community to 'others'

outside the church in order to ensure civil order by "major consent"—majority rule—on

"civil things" for the public good of the entire community.[42] This differentiates between

the unanimous individual consent required to establish a community and the majority

consent required to establish a government to govern the community.

---

[39] Lutz, 28.

[40] Ibid., 28, 81.

[41] Bruce Frohnen, *The American Republic: Primary Sources,* ed. Bruce Frohnen (Indianapolis: Liberty Fund, 2002) Chapter: *Providence Agreement August 20, 1637,* http://oll.libertyfund.org/title/669/206080 (Accessed February 27, 2012).

[42] Lutz, 28.

As colonies combined and grew larger, the first functional *constitutions* were developed by combining covenants, compacts and charters. As an example, the Pilgrim Code of Law of 1636 combined the Mayflower Compact with the royal charter to constitute a legal political covenant with England. Included in the document was a detailed description of local political institutions, which centered on the representative legislature that governed by popular consent. This inclusion of the political institutions that constitute the government in the document delineated the Pilgrim Code of Law as the first—albeit elementary—modern *constitution,* which began the American tradition of constitutionalism.[43]

Just three years later, "the first written constitution of modern democracy" was developed in the Fundamental Orders of Connecticut of 1639, which was later chartered by the British Crown in 1662.[44] This constitution represented a unique compact to govern a federation of communities. The residents of Windsor, Hartford and Wethersfield agreed to combine their communities together in a federation as one "state or commonwealth."[45] The *federal* system referred to here is simply another covenant between the individual communities. In fact, the Latin root for the English word "federal" is *foedus,* which means "covenant."[46] However, the key to the federal system is that each town government continued to function, but a representative body called the "General Court" was established to act as the "supreme power of the Commonwealth."[47] The rest of the towns in Connecticut slowly joined the confederation. In 1662, Charles II

---

[43] Ibid., 27.

[44] Huntington, *Who Are We?,* 43.

[45] Lutz, 47.

[46] Ibid., 43.

[47] Ibid.

ratified the federal system in a formal charter, which gave Connecticut legal status as a self-governed colony. The Connecticut Charter of 1662 represents the "convergence of colonial constitutional documents, compacts and charters, into the American style of *constitution*."[48] Rhode Island developed a similar constitutional style document and was granted a similar charter in 1663.

The American colonies effectively used covenants, compacts, and charters to provide local government to the colonies. In the course of this political experimentation from 1620 to 1639, the isolated communities throughout New England developed a historically significant political idea—"the written constitution, found in a single document and adopted by the citizens through their direct consent."[49]   A little more than twenty years later, the colonies of Connecticut and Rhode Island developed a working federal constitution with a colonial-designed local popular government that was legally recognized by the British Crown through a charter. These foundational documents, which were developed by necessity from the colonists' own religious and political traditions, served as the foundation of America's constitutional tradition that was further refined through the practical experience of the colonists and passed on to the Founding Fathers.[50]

---

[48] Ibid., 47.

[49] Ibid., 27.

[50] Ibid., 31. English common law, the Magna Carta (1215) and the Petition of Right (1628) undoubtedly influenced these political documents. However, some have argued that these documents and the principles underlying them merely represent a "synthesis of European Whig and Enlightenment thinkers." It is certainly true that the Founding Fathers frequently cited Montesquieu, Blackstone and Locke during the development of the Constitution in the late eighteenth century. However, these influential thinkers could not have had any influence on the foundational colonial documents culminating in the Fundamental Orders of Connecticut, since Locke was still a child in 1639 and neither Montesquieu nor Blackstone had even been born.

The first two constitutions that formed the foundations for the state constitutions were "covenants or compacts written by the colonists"—The Pilgrim Code of Law of 1636 and the Fundamental Orders of Connecticut of 1639. However, the two functional constitutions that followed were legally granted as charters—The Connecticut (1662) and Rhode Island (1663) Charters.[51] All are representative of the developing American political theory and constitutional tradition that combined elements of covenants, compacts and charters to develop and establish effective self-governance in the American colonies, which protected civil liberty and maintained civil order.[52] Therefore, more than a century before the Constitution, parts of the colonies had already developed and instituted most of the basic elements of American political theory: popular sovereignty, federalism, the republican form of government, and a constitution to define political institutions. The American communities continued to consolidate into larger federated colonies, as well as develop and refine their governments, but they were still just a collection of British colonies on the North American continent.

The Political Transformation to the United States of America

Despite the incredible political and constitutional developments that progressed within the colonies, independence from Britain required the creation of new state and federal constitutions to establish the foundation for a true American national community and government. "Prior to the 1760s, there was "no 'people' that could properly be called American."[53] The thirteen colonies largely consisted of a collection of separate

---

[51] Ibid., 38.

[52] Ibid.

[53] Ibid., 7.

federated communities that had consolidated independently within each colony. However, the large federated communities that made up each of the original colonies were well established. As the war of independence began, the thirteen colonies were relatively uniform and consolidated with over 90 percent of the colonists living in well established and harmonious communities, most of which had been steadily growing for more than a century.[54] However, the colonies quickly unified and declared their independence together as *a people* in the Declaration of Independence when the hostilities with the British Crown erupted into the Revolutionary War. Despite the fact that the Tories, a small minority faction loyal to the British, opposed revolution, the relative strength and stability of this widespread unity across the colonies led to America's emergence as *a people*. This strong unity was enabled in part by the unprecedented homogeneity of their Anglo-American Protestant culture, which established the common interests, values, and rights that unified the national community.

The Foundation for Unity: Anglo-American/Protestant Culture

In large measure, the rapid American political development in the "1770s and 1780s was rooted in, and a product of, the Anglo-American Protestant culture that had developed over the intervening one and a half centuries."[55] America was a "highly homogenous society in terms of race, national origin, and religion."[56] Since America was settled almost exclusively by Europeans, the "white population was ethnically 60 percent English, 80 percent British (the remainder being largely German and Dutch), and *98*

---

[54] Ibid., 71.

[55] Huntington, *Who we Are?*, 40.

[56] Ibid., 44.

percent Protestant."[57] John Jay also based the unity of the Americans on their common

ancestry, language, beliefs, and culture in *The Federalist Papers.*

> Providence has been pleased to give this one connected country to one
> united people—a people descended from the same ancestors, speaking the
> same language, professing the same religion, attached to the same
> principles of government, very similar in manners and customs, and who,
> by their joint counsels, arms, and efforts, fighting side by side throughout
> a long and bloody war, have nobly established their general liberty and
> independence.[58]

In this context, "Jay undoubtedly meant Protestantism" by his statement that one united

people professed the "same religion."[59] Huntington equates the values of American

culture with secularized ideas based on their common religion. "The American Creed, in

short, is Protestantism without God, the secular credo of the 'nation with the soul of a

church.'"[60]

Religion had a tremendous influence in the consent-based communitarian political

structure of America, because individual *morality* balanced individual *freedom* with

obedience and civil *rights* with *responsibilities.* This was achieved through a healthy

balance between church and state that promoted unity, as well as, civil liberty and order.

Alexis de Tocqueville, after his 1831 visit observed in his famous classic, *Democracy in

America,* that religion should be "regarded as the first of their political institutions,"

---

[57] Ibid.

[58] Alexander Hamilton, James Madison, and John Jay, *The Federalist Papers*, ed. Clint Rossiter, (New York: New American Library, 2003), 32.

[59] Huntington, *Who we Are?*, 60.

[60] Ibid., 63, 69. Huntington concludes: "Scholars who attempt to identify the American 'liberal consensus' or Creed solely with Lockeian ideas and enlightenment are giving a secular interpretation to the religious sources of American values."

despite the fact that it "never interferes directly in the government of Americans."[61] This enigma intrigued Tocqueville, because in France the "spirit of religion" opposed the "spirit of freedom" because of the corruption of power in the political combination of the Church and the state, which was common throughout Europe. However, in America, he found the spirit of religion and freedom "linked together in joint reign over the same land," which "all attributed the peaceful influence exercised by religion over their country principally to the *separation of Church and state.*"[62] However, the intent of this separation of Church and state was not to "establish freedom *from* religion but to establish freedom *for* religion."[63] Religion did not reign through political power in America. Therefore, it was free to reign in each individual's heart, mind and soul by his own consent and reign by consent in their communities through the *morality* of the people. Because of the central role of individual and community *consent*, Tocqueville viewed religion as the foundation for national unity and the spring of civil liberty and order. [64] In America, religion and morality was in balance with the nation's law, which promoted harmony between the people and the government. Therefore, religion and morality supported civil liberty, by balancing individual *freedom* with *obedience* and civil *rights* with civil *responsibilities*.

---

[61] Alexis De Tocqueville, *Democracy in America,* trans. Gerald E. Bevan (London: Penguin Books Ltd., 1971), 342.

[62] Tocqueville, 345.

[63] Huntington, *Who are We?,* 85.

[64] Tocqueville, 340-1. "Christianity reigns without obstacles by universal consent," since "all the sects in the United States unite in the body of Christendom whose morality is everywhere the same" with universal agreement on the "duties that men owe to each other."

The symbiotic relationship between religion and civil liberty created balance in America because personal *morality* was in harmony with and essential to *civil order*. George Washington confirmed this critical point in his second Farewell Address.

> Of all the dispositions and habits which lead to political prosperity, religion and morality are indispensable supports. In vain would that man claim the tribute of patriotism, who should labor to subvert these great pillars of human happiness, these *firmest props of the duties of men and citizens*. The mere politician, equally with the pious man, ought to respect and to cherish them….It is substantially true that virtue or *morality* is a *necessary spring of popular government*.[65]

American religion and morality were critical supports to the balance between civil liberty and order because they were a powerful check and balance on the *depravity of human nature* to empower the necessary "duties of men and citizens" required in popular government.[66] Given the conflicting self-interests common to human nature, it is difficult to envision sustaining civil liberty and order through *consent*, without such a uniform and homogenous religious culture that not only supported civil liberty and order, but also *empowered* it.

The problem confronting the Founding Fathers was to create a government that provided the civil liberty to foster and promote the religious freedom and morality of the American people, but also possessed the power to mitigate the risk to civil order by the depravity of human nature. The grand strategy was to utilize American political theory to

---

[65] George Washington, Avalon Project: Documents in Law, History and Diplomacy, "George Washington's Farewell Address, 1796," Lillian Goldman Law Library, Yale Law School, http://avalon.law.yale.edu/18th_century/washing.asp (accessed September 20, 2011). "And let us with caution indulge the supposition that morality can be maintained without religion. Whatever may be conceded to the influence of refined education on minds of peculiar structure, reason and experience both forbid us to expect that national morality can prevail in exclusion of religious principle….Promote then, as an object of primary importance, institutions for the general diffusion of knowledge. In proportion as the structure of a government gives force to public opinion, it is essential that public opinion should be enlightened."

[66] Tocqueville, 56. "Liberty looks upon religion as its companion in its struggles and triumphs, as the cradle of its young life, as the divine source of its claims. It considers religion as the guardian of morality, morality as the guarantee of law and the security that freedom will last."

develop and establish an innovative institutional government that was granted the power to check and balance human nature in both the population and the government in order to ensure civil order, without jeopardizing civil liberty. The Founding Fathers combined the rich traditions of American political development with practical political theory, which, after a great deal of trial and error, effectively forged the sovereign states together under the stable federal republic of the United States. The final result was America's founding documents—the Declaration of Independence, the State Constitutions and the U.S. Constitution.

Declaration of Independence

In 1776, America's Founding Fathers codified the 'self-evident truth' of the underlying principles of liberty and order in America's first national compact as *a people*, The Declaration of Independence. "We hold these truths to be self-evident, that all men are created equal, that they are endowed by their Creator with certain inalienable Rights, that among those are Life, Liberty and the pursuit of Happiness.—That to secure these rights, Governments are instituted among Men, deriving their just powers from the consent of the governed." As equals before their Creator, colonial Americans had united themselves by consent to form a national community based on common values, rights and interests. In order to secure their rights in these communities, they also had to institute an effective republican government with sufficient power to enforce civil order without jeopardizing their hard won civil liberty.

"The Declaration of Independence together with the first national constitution, the Articles of Confederation, were the American's first national compact."[67] In the

---

[67] Lutz, 112.

American constitutional tradition, this compact created a people and a government, including a definition of basic values. At the time, the Articles of Confederation codified the "institutions for collective decision making" to define the mechanism of government, which met the requirement for a constitution.[68] When the Articles of Confederation required modification, the compact that defined America as *a people* remained in effect. Therefore, the Declaration of Independence remained the nation's compact after the U.S. Constitution replaced the Articles of Confederation.[69]

State Constitutions

Due to the common core culture, the thirteen states that emerged from these colonies developed separate state "constitutions quite similar in form and content" utilizing a "common, coherent theory" as the foundation, which was associated with the Whigs—"Anti-Federalists."[70] The various forms of self-government each of the original thirteen colonies independently created were "highly congruent and surprisingly easy to synthesize into a system" of state and national government.[71] However, these state constitutions are part of the same American constitutional tradition, which was modified by the "Federalist" Founding Fathers to design the federal republican form of government described in the U.S. Constitution.[72]

After declaring independence, the Founding Fathers continued the constitutional tradition by developing founding documents at the state and national level with

---

[68] Ibid., 111.

[69] Ibid., 112.

[70] Ibid.

[71] Ibid., 7.

[72] Ibid., 96.

"compacts that contained constitutions" in order to formalize popular sovereignty in America.[73] Independence enabled the colonial constitutional traditions to take the next logical step in self-government. "The Crown was no longer sovereign; the people were. The Crown did not make unilateral agreements based on asymmetrical power; the people did."[74] True *popular sovereignty* came of age in America. At the request of the Second Continental Congress in 1775, State Constitutions began to be drafted to "establish some form of government independent of the British Crown."[75] The colonial tradition of constitutionalism matured further between 1776 and 1787 in the development of multiple iterations of the state constitutions, the national Articles of Confederation, and ultimately, the U.S. Constitution.[76] Therefore, the state constitutions are "part of the national document and are needed to complete the legal text" because collectively they provided the "foundation upon which the United States Constitution rests."[77] However, unlike the U.S. Constitution, the Articles of Confederation created a national government that could not effectively govern the sovereign states.

The Articles of Confederation

The Articles of Confederation became a failed experiment because it created a weak national government with insufficient power to maintain order among the sovereign states to effectively promote *national* interests. The Articles represented a compact of sovereign states to enter into a "firm *league* of friendship with each other, for

---

[73] Ibid., 112.

[74] Ibid., 152.

[75] Ibid., 100.

[76] Ibid., 5.

[77] Ibid., 96.

their common defense, the security of their liberties, and their mutual and general welfare."[78] However, divergent state interests created factions that divided national interests and confused national action. These state factions also made the nation vulnerable to the manipulation of foreign powers, which still had imperial interests in America. The basic problem was that the Articles of Confederation granted no legitimate authority or power to the national government. Therefore, the Articles depended completely on the unity and consent of the sovereign states to be effective. The national government was not granted the sovereign authority to properly check state interests or enforce national law—similar to the design of the League of Nations or the United Nations at the international level.

The Articles of Confederation established a national government that lacked the true popular sovereignty to govern the people directly or enforce the law according to the *national* interest. The confederate government did not directly represent the people in accordance with popular sovereignty.[79] The Articles of Confederation limited both representation and sovereignty to the states. Only the states could pass laws that directly affected the people, since the people did not directly elect the Confederate government. The "national legislature could not act directly upon the citizens of states" because the Articles represented a "compact among the states," not with the people.[80] However, unlike the rules of colonial communities, the states did not consent to majority rule under the Articles of Confederation. The states retained their full sovereignty over their

---

[78] Articles of Confederation, Avalon Project: Documents in Law, History and Diplomacy, "Articles of Confederation: March 1, 1781," Lillian Goldman Law Library, Yale Law School, http://avalon.law.yale.edu/18th_century/artconf.asp (accessed September 20, 2011)

[79] Hamilton, Madison, and Jay, 103, 108.

[80] Lutz, 64, 151.

citizens and designated *national representatives* to represent *state interests*. Each state governed their citizens in accordance with the interests of the state. The national government did not have the authority or sovereignty to provide the requisite check on state interests to determine, promote, and enforce *national* interests. The "concurrence of thirteen distinct sovereign wills" was required "under the Confederation" to enact or execute any domestic or foreign policy. However, in accordance with the interest-driven reality of human nature, "Each State yielding to the persuasive voice of immediate interest or convenience" withdrew the support required for necessary action.[81] Thus, *national* policy was ineffective because any one state could effectively veto a decision based on competing state interests. The national government did not have sufficient authority or power to promote and secure *national* interests.

Ultimately, the institutional design of the Articles of Confederation did not provide the essential balance of civil liberty and order required for an effective national government. In *The Federalist Papers*, Hamilton describes the only real alternative to an effective government over men to establish order—military force against sovereign states or nations, which was unacceptable.

> Government implies the power of making laws. It is essential to the idea of a law that it be attended with a sanction; or in other words, a penalty or punishment for disobedience. If there be no penalty annexed to disobedience, the resolutions or commands which pretend to be laws will, in fact, amount to nothing more than advice or recommendation. This penalty, whatever it may be, can only be inflicted in two ways: by the agency of the courts and ministers of justice, or by military force; by the COERCION of the magistracy, or by the COERCION of arms. The first kind can evidently apply only to men; the last kind must of necessity be employed against bodies politic, or communities, or States.[82]

---

[81] Hamilton, Madison, and Jay, 107-8

[82] Ibid., 105.

Civil order was difficult to achieve under the Articles without the threat of a civil war between the states. Hamilton concludes with his verdict on the Articles of Confederation:

> Experience is the oracle of truth; and where its responses are unequivocal; they ought to be conclusive and sacred. The important truth, which unequivocally pronounces in the present case, is that a sovereignty over sovereigns, a government over governments, a legislation <u>for</u> <u>communities,</u> as counterdistinguished <u>from individuals,</u> as it is a solecism [absurdity] in theory, so in practice it is subversive of the *order* and ends of civil polity, by substituting *violence* in place of the mild and salutatory *coercion* of the *magistracy* [government].[83]

Therefore, the Articles of Confederation, as a league or compact of sovereign states, did not constitute an effective government to establish civil liberty and order and would have likely led to a civil war. Thus, the leading men in American politics, the Founding Fathers, were charged to address these problems in the Constitutional Convention.

The Constitution of the United States

The Constitutional Convention was formed in 1787 to deliberate on a new Constitution for the United States in order to replace the ineffective Articles of Confederation. The Founding Fathers clearly understood the difficulty in establishing an effective government that maintained the delicate balance between civil liberty and civil order because their first national constitution had failed.[84] As the disunity of state interests were "drawing rapidly to a crisis" in 1786, George Washington explained that the core reason the strategic design of the Articles of Confederation was ineffective was due to an idealistic assumption in their strategy to establish an effective government. He traced the fundamental cause of the problem to a *flawed assumption* of *human nature* and

---

[83] Hamilton, Madison, and Jay, 133. This verdict equally applies to the similar, more modern *international* organizations, such as the League of Nations and United Nations, which will be discussed in the next chapter.

[84] Ibid., 27.

advocated for a stronger national government to check human nature through coercive

power.

> We have errors to correct; we have probably had too good an opinion of *human nature* in forming our confederation. Experience has taught us, that men will not adopt and carry into execution measures the best calculated for their own good, without the intervention of a *coercive power*. I do not conceive we can exist long as a nation without having lodged some where a power, which will pervade the whole Union in as energetic a manner, as the authority of the State Governments extends over the several States....We must take *human nature* as we find it: perfection falls not to the share of mortals.[85]

Therefore, the Constitution had to mitigate the strategic risk posed by human nature to

develop an effective institutional design for government at the national level.

The mission of the 1787 Constitutional Convention was to form a stronger, more

effective *republican* form of government by correcting this flawed assumption in order to

mitigate the strategic risk that practical experience had exposed.[86] However, the

Founding Fathers were also well aware of the problems and instability of historic

republics. In *The Federalist Papers*, Alexander Hamilton recounts the "history of the

petty republics of Athens and Italy" that "were kept in a state of perpetual vibration

between the extremes of tyranny and anarchy." The "disorders of these republics" have

enabled "advocates of despotism" to argue against the "very principles of civil liberty"

---

[85] *The Writings of George Washington from the Original Manuscript Sources*, ed. John C. Fitzpatrick (Washington: United States Printing Office, 1931-1944), Vol. 28, 502-3, University of Virginia Library electronic text, under "To THE SECRETARY OF FOREIGN AFFAIRS [Mount Vernon, August 1, 1786]," http://etext.virginia.edu/etcbin/toccer-new2?id=WasFi28.xml&images=images/modeng&data=/texts/english/modeng/parsed&tag=public&part=394&division=div1 (accessed February 29, 2012).

[86] Hamilton, Madison, and Jay, 76. A *republic* or the *republican* form of government centered on the delegation of governmental power to a select group of citizens elected by the people to govern them as representatives and stewards of the people's popular sovereignty.

and "all free government as inconsistent with the order of society."[87] The Articles of Confederation had already proven to be a failed experiment. However, it had not been properly designed, since it was hurriedly put into place under duress in the midst of the Revolutionary War.

The Founding Fathers were confident that an innovative institutional design could be used to mitigate the tyranny associated with human nature. The federalists were confident that "human ingenuity could devise mechanisms that would at once protect liberty, allow effective government, and rest on the consent of the people."[88] Alexander Hamilton explains the common sentiment at the Convention: "[I]t seems to have been reserved to the people of this country, by their conduct and example, to decide the important question, whether societies of men are really capable or not of establishing good government from reflection and choice, or whether they are forever destined to depend for their political constitutions on accident and force."[89] Human ingenuity was required to design an innovative government institution that provided a powerful and effective check on human nature to channel the government and the population without resorting to tyranny.

James Madison explained the enduring challenge of constructing good government in the context of the reality of human nature. "In framing a government which is to be administered by men over men, the great difficulty lies in this: you must first enable the government to control the governed [civil order]; and in the next place

---

[87] Ibid., 66.

[88] Ralph Ketcham, ed., *The Anti-Federalist Papers and the Constitutional Convention Debates* (New York: New American Library, 2003), 15.

[89] Hamilton, Madison, and Jay, 27.

oblige it to control itself" to protect civil liberty.[90] Based on the heated debates at Constitutional Convention, this was a difficult balance to strike. However, after much debate, the Founding Fathers developed the Constitution of the United States, which drew upon a modified and refined American (federalist) political theory to design an effective government that could provide a stable balance between civil liberty and order despite the challenges associated with human nature.

The enduring effectiveness of the Constitution and the United States of America is strong evidence that the strategy of government developed by the Founding Fathers was based on realistic assumptions and valid strategic logic, which effectively mitigated the risk of human nature. The two most significant factors contributing to the strategic success of the U.S. Constitution were: 1) the homogeneity of the American community, consisting of a unified common core Anglo-American Protestant culture; and 2) the innovative political theory based on popular sovereignty used to design the U.S. Constitution. The significant importance of the homogeneity of Anglo-American Protestant culture in integrating American communities together as a united people has already been discussed. America's political theory of popular sovereignty formed the theoretical foundation for the Constitution. However, the Founding Fathers also combined other innovative, but practical, theoretical designs to establish a government institution that protected America's civil liberty from the risk of future tyranny and despotism. These were well known to be a constant feature in human government based on the depravity of human nature.

---

[90] Ibid., 319.

American Political Theory

The U.S. Constitution was the culmination of over a century and a half of political

thought and practice in America. The rich backdrop of Western Civilization, European

Enlightenment, as well as English common law and political theory certainly influenced

political thought in America. However, America added immeasurably to the Western

Civilization tradition through a unique form of American political theory and the tradition

of constitutionalism. The Founding Fathers exercised great wisdom and judgment in

designing the U.S. Constitution on the solid and realistic foundation of American political

theory, which had been shaped and refined by the lessons of history and practical

American experience. The effectiveness of the U.S. Constitution centered on four major

theoretical concepts: 1) popular sovereignty; 2) federalism; 3) extended republic; and 4)

the separation of powers with checks and balances.

Popular Sovereignty: The Theoretical Balance of Civil Liberty and Order

The central concept of American political theory is *popular sovereignty*—the

political idea that "the *community* and its *government* originate in the *consent* of the

people," which is the foundation of *civil liberty.* [91] *Popular sovereignty* created and

sustained *civil liberty* through the symbiotic consensual relationship created between the

people, the *community*, and the *government*, which balanced natural liberty with

obedience and civil rights with responsibilities. *Civil liberty* represented the balance

between liberty and order. The symbiotic consensual relationship began with the people,

who transferred their inherent *power*—sovereignty—to the community by *consent.* The

people agreed it was in their *interests* to join a community and consented to restrict their

---

[91] Lutz, 81.

natural liberty and accept the *civil responsibility* to obey and submit to the *majority rule* of the community based on common *values,* which formed the foundation for *civil liberty.* *Communities* were formed by *consent* of the *people* through a *compact*, which was a two-part agreement: 1) the individual *unanimous* agreement to form the community and submit to the *majority rule* of the collective community; and 2) a *majority* agreement on the type of government that will govern the community. In order to secure *civil liberty,* the community collectively instituted government by *majority consent* via a *compact* to enforce *civil order* through *laws* and *institutions* defined in a constitution in order to protect *civil rights.* Therefore, *popular sovereignty* represented the fundamental political theory in America and served as the foundational means in the Unites States for the people to transfer *power* and *sovereignty* by *consent* to the community and the government, which has sustained the *balance between liberty and order—*see Figure 1.

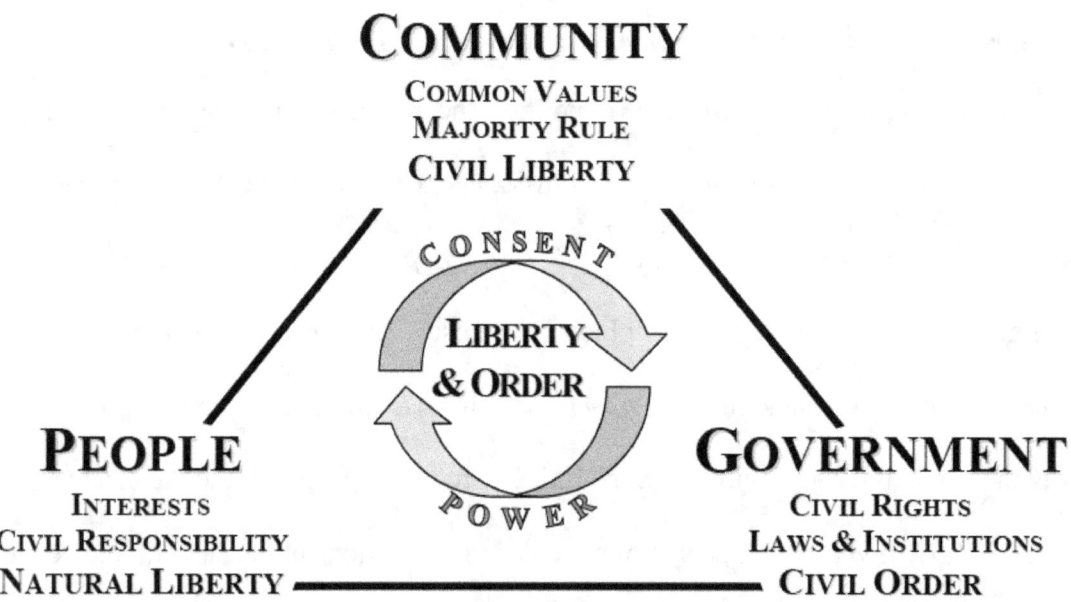

Figure 1: Theoretical Model of American Popular Sovereignty

Additionally, the Founding Fathers used institutional political theory to institute popular sovereignty in America at the national level, as well as mitigate the risk posed by human nature.

The Institutional Political Theory of the U.S. Constitution

Popular sovereignty was combined with three institutional design theories to develop an innovative and balanced strategic design, which effectively mitigated the fundamental strategic *risk* to the long-term balance between civil liberty and order—the *depravity of human nature.* The primary threat was the *tyranny of factions*, which is "sown in the nature of man."[92] The factions of most concern were the tyranny of the government and the majority.[93] Though self-government based on popular sovereignty assumed a virtuous people, the Founding Fathers had a realistic view of human nature based on experience. Government abuse of power was too prevalent in history and experience to ignore. Additionally, the majority rule inherent with governments based on popular sovereignty could be used for the majority to oppress a minority unjustly or lead to a minority faction resorting to violence in order to fight the injustice. The Founding Fathers knew that the "causes of faction cannot be removed," so the solution was to establish the "means of controlling its *effects*."[94] Therefore, the strategy was to "break and control the violence of the faction" in order to mitigate the strategic risk of tyranny through the innovative use of institutional design.[95]

---

[92] Hamilton, Madison, and Jay, 73. Lutz, 84. The tyranny of factions is defined as "the arbitrary use of power" wielded by a number of citizens, whether amounting to a majority or minority of the whole, who are united and actuated by some common impulse of passion, or of interest, adverse to the rights of other citizens, or to the permanent and aggregate interests of the community."

[93] Lutz, 86., Hamilton, Madison, and Jay, 76-7, 320.

[94] Hamilton, Madison, and Jay, 75.

[95] Ibid., 71.

The Founding Fathers utilized the *republican* form of government because it was the most effective form to institute popular sovereignty, as well as mitigate the *tyranny of the majority* through the representative legislature. The *republican* form of government delegated governmental power to a select group of citizens—*representatives*—elected by the people to represent them as stewards of the people's popular sovereignty. In contrast, a democracy is a "society consisting of a small number of citizens, who assemble and administer the government in person," which have historically been "spectacles of turbulence and contention" because a democracy possesses "no cure for the mischiefs of faction" that result in violence against the minority.[96] However, in a republic, *representative legislatures* were the first check on the tyranny of the majority. The legislature represented "all interests within the community in due proportion" through elected representatives.[97] However, the true power of the republican form was that the legislature—through a "highly deliberative process"—collectively manifested the wisdom and judgment to govern the people in the "true interest of the country" without violating minority rights or compromising majority interests for temporary gains.[98] Therefore, the representative legislatures were designed to provide a check to majority tyranny, by protecting the minority, in order to secure the blessings of civil liberty and order for the majority and minority alike.

---

[96] Hamilton, Madison, and Jay, 76. The republican form was favored in both the colonies and the states as demonstrated by the representative nature and legislative supremacy of all their forms of government.

[97] Lutz, 95.

[98] Hamilton, Madison, and Jay, 76. Lutz, 85. "The fundamental strategy for controlling the evil of faction is delay. Make it difficult for a majority to form, and require its expression in an arena dominated by more virtuous men."

The Founding Fathers used *federalism* to institute popular sovereignty in the national and state governments to enable an extended republic to be effectively governed, which provided a check to both the tyranny of the government and the majority. *Federalism* defined how the people granted and delineated their popular sovereignty to the state and national government. In accordance with popular sovereignty, the U.S. Constitution recognized the "dual citizenship" of the people as members of both a sovereign nation and sovereign states.[99] The citizens were subject to both state and federal authority and laws based on consent, since the people directly elected state and national representatives in the legislatures. A bicameral legislature was designed to represent the interests of the people and the states. The House of Representatives represents the people; the Senate represents the states. Since the people directly elect members of the House of Representatives, the Congress can pass laws directly affecting the people in accordance with popular sovereignty. The division of power between state and national governments, and the provision for dual legislatures at each level also created a balance of power to provide a check on governmental tyranny. Federalism also enabled a check on majority tyranny via an extended republic.

The combination of the republican form and federal design provided the capability to govern an *extended republic* by maintaining sufficient state power and sovereignty to govern each state effectively as the republic expanded. Tocqueville remarked that the "sovereignty of the Union is a work of art. The sovereignty of the states is natural, autonomous, effortless like a father's control over his family," which enabled the national government to govern an extended republic of united states

---

[99] Lutz., 153.

effectively.[100] The large population and the diverse interests of the *extended republic* was intended to prevent the formation of a natural majority.[101] A collaborative deliberative process was required to consolidate a coalition of minorities in order to constitute a true majority.[102] As the competing interests of various minorities interacted, the legislature collectively made decisions for the "greatest good for the greatest number" through the deliberative process of agreement, compromise and accommodation.[103] Thus, the collective virtue and wisdom of the nation was externally bolstered through the extended republic because government representatives were forced to take into account minority interests in the long-term interests of the nation. The extended republic design was an effective institutional design to mitigate the tyranny of the majority and the violence that could potentially arise in the minority. This mitigation of tyranny was critical in maintaining the long-term equilibrium between civil liberty and order.

The Constitution also fractured the concentration of power in the government through *separation of powers, checks,* and *balances* to prevent the governmental tyranny common to human government.[104] The powers of government were separated into three branches of government—the Executive, Legislative, and Judicial Branch—though each branch was interdependent on the others to effectively govern. The separation of judicial authority from the executive branch was a particular American innovation.[105] The "fragmentation of sovereignty" maintained the "balance of power" to mitigate human

---

[100] Tocqueville, 196.

[101] Hamilton, Madison, and Jay, 321.

[102] Ibid., 320-21.

[103] Lutz, 156.

[104] Hamilton, Madison, and Jay, 320., Lutz, 156.

[105] Lutz, 157.

nature within the government because "ambition effectively counteracts ambition."[106]

The balance of power existed between the federal and state governments, as well as, between the three branches of federal government. The balance of power was designed to favor the federal government to ensure effectiveness, but the states were powerful enough to collectively act as a check on federal power. Likewise, the balance of power between the three branches of government was in favor of the Legislative Branch because of the supremacy of the legislature in the American tradition, based on republican nature of popular sovereignty.[107] Government powers were separated in order to prevent any individual or faction from gaining too much power, which could be used to threaten the civil liberty of the people. This is in keeping with the "historical truth epitomized in Lord Acton's famous dictum: 'All power corrupts, and absolute power corrupts absolutely'."[108]

Similarly, *checks* force the interdependent governmental functions to work together in a deliberative process in order to effectively govern, which provides a further check on branch power.[109] Legislative supremacy was also designed into the checks, since the legislative branch was granted the most authority to check the other branches. For instance, the executive veto is a check on the legislative branch, but the legislature was granted authority to override the veto with a two-thirds majority. The legislature also checks the executive branch in foreign policy, since the Senate must confirm Ambassadors and ratify treaties initiated by the President. However, the ultimate

---

[106] Tocqueville, 196., Lutz, 156.

[107] Lutz, 156.

[108] B. H. Liddell Hart, *Strategy* (New York: Penguin Group, 1991), 354.

[109] Lutz, 157-8.

legislative check on the consolidation of power by the other branches is the congressional budget authority—the power of the purse.

Balances in the constitutional design of the government also limit the consolidation of power across branches. The primary balance is provided by the diverse terms of office in each of the branches.[110] The staggered terms of office across the branches—the President (4 years), Senate (6 years), and the House of Representatives (2 years)—requires that any faction must gain and hold a majority for a sustained period of time to consolidate significant governmental influence and power through elections. The constituency of each of the offices is also different, which further fractures any efforts to consolidate power or influence. These balances focus electoral influence towards the strongest long-term majority interests of the American people. Ultimately, this system of balances is designed to prevent any one minority or government faction from gaining control across branches or departments.[111] These institutional separations, checks, and balances force the government to utilize a deliberative process to govern, which prevents the consolidation of political power and mitigates the risk of governmental tyranny, which would lead to the loss of American civil liberty.

In conclusion, the Constitution operates as an effective grand strategy for maintaining the balance between liberty and order through civil liberty in the United States. The Founding Fathers developed an effective and enduring Constitution by using *institutional design to channel human nature to govern effectively and prevent tyranny in the government.*[112] The innovative combination of institutional mechanisms effectively

---

[110] Ibid., 163.

[111] Ibid., 164.

[112] Ibid., 165.

instituted popular sovereignty and checked both majority and governmental tyranny, which mitigated the strategic risk and consequences of the depravity of human nature common in all governments and societies. The Constitution instituted *popular sovereignty* through *republican government*, subjecting the people only to laws based on their consent—laws passed by the majority of elected representatives through the legislature.[113] The Constitution also instituted *federalism*, in conjunction with the *separation of powers*, *checks*, and *balances* in order to provide a "double security" for civil liberty. The federal and state governments balance and check each other in addition to the internal checks and balances within each government.[114] *Federalism* also enabled the creation of an *extended republic* which fractured the tyranny of the majority. Alexander Hamilton explained the purpose of the extended republic: "society itself will be broken into so many parts, interests and classes of citizens, that the rights of individuals, or of the minority, will be in little danger from interested combinations of the majority."[115]

The Declaration of Independence, together with the Preamble to the Constitution, form the nation's compact that creates *a people* and defines their national identity. The U.S. Constitution provides the institutional framework to exercise popular sovereignty through a republican federal government. Elected representatives exercise collective wisdom and judgment through a deliberative process to govern an extended republic. Ultimately, the Constitution has established a government that has maintained civil

---

[113] Ibid., 155.

[114] Hamilton, Madison, and Jay, 320. These institutional mechanisms effectively mitigate *governmental tyranny* because "the power surrendered by the people is first divided between two distinct governments [state and national], and then a portion allotted to each subdivided among distinct and separate departments [executive, legislative and judicial]."

[115] Ibid., 321.

liberty and order for the good of the American people. Therefore, the Constitution is
essential and effective foundation of America's grand strategy.

CHAPTER 3: HISTORICAL CRITICISM OF AMERICAN GRAND STRATEGY

America's First and Enduring Grand Strategy

The founding documents—The Declaration of Independence and the Constitution of the United States—constitute America's first and enduring grand strategy to secure liberty and order. This grand strategy continues to be effective, as well as a *valid* strategy that is *suitable*, *acceptable*, and *feasible*. The founding documents remain *suitable* because they are still effective at maintaining America's civil liberty and sustaining civil order, despite severe challenges in the past such as the Civil War. The Constitution is still *acceptable* because it has maintained the approval and support of both the people and the States, as amended. The Constitution remains *feasible* because the *means* provided to the government continue to be sufficient to achieve the nation's strategic *ends*. The key to the *effectiveness* and longevity of America's first and enduring grand strategy is that the Founding Fathers grounded it on practical wisdom, sound *assumptions*, and a realistic assessment and mitigation of *risk*.

The Founding Fathers' innovative design provided an institutional balance of power in the Constitution, which was based on a realistic *assumption* concerning human nature. The Founding Fathers were completely realistic about human nature and "were under no illusions about the corruptible nature of men and governments."[1] George Washington, who served a leading role as a Founding Father, was certainly grounded in

---

[1] Walter A. McDougall, *Promised Land, Crusader State: The American Encounter with the World Since 1776* (New York: Houghton Mifflin Company, 1997), 26.

the truth about the "depravity of human nature" based on the clear lessons of history and his own hard won personal experience.

> It is vain to exclaim against the *depravity of human nature* on this account; the fact is so, the experience of every age and nation has proved it and we must in a great measure, change the constitution of man, before we can make it otherwise. *No institution, not built on the presumptive truth of these maxims can succeed.* [2]

Therefore, the Founding Fathers designed the institutional structure of the American government within the Constitution to mitigate the risk posed by human nature through the institutional use of separation of powers, checks, and balances. However, the impacts of human nature also had to be mitigated in the international environment. The U.S. Constitution was also designed to create sufficient central authority to balance and check foreign power, and defend America against *foreign aggression*. However, the military power required to defend the nation could also be used to oppress the people. The Constitution, as American grand strategy, had to reconcile the critical need for military power to defend against foreign threats abroad with the internal threat that military power posed to liberty at home. The Constitution defines the ends-ways-means of grand strategy and grants sufficient authority and power to execute it effectively, while also establishing checks and balances to prevent those powers from being abused—a balance of power that enabled the government to defend the nation and maintain civil order, without endangering the civil liberties of the people.[3]

---

[2] *The Writings of George Washington from the Original Manuscript Sources*, ed. John C. Fitzpatrick (Washington: United States Printing Office, 1931-1944), Vol. 10, 363, University of Virginia Library electronic text, under "To THE COMMITTEE OF CONGRESSWITH THE ARMY27 [Head Quarters, January 29, 1778.]," http://etext.virginia.edu/washington/fitzpatrick/ (accessed February 29, 2012).

[3] McDougall, *Promised Land, Crusader State*, 26.

The Ends of American Grand Strategy

The vital national interests, which also define the *ends* of America's first grand strategy, are detailed in the Preamble of the Constitution. The primary end was to "establish this Constitution for the United States of America." The United States government executed the remaining ends outlined in the Preamble in accordance with the Constitution: "form a more perfect Union, establish Justice, insure Domestic Tranquility, provide for the common defence, promote the general Welfare, and secure the Blessings of Liberty to Ourselves and our Posterity." The Founding Fathers determined that these strategic ends would enable America to establish and sustain civil liberty and order in the context of the strategic environment. However, foreign policy ends are addressed only from the limited perspective of defending America from foreign power and influence.[4] This is in keeping with the true nature of civil liberty and order. The government was focused on protecting American liberty at home from both foreign and domestic enemies versus projecting liberty abroad. Therefore, these strategic *ends* remain relevant in the current strategic environment, because they are essential to the vital national interests of the United States. Thus, the U.S. Constitution is still effective as the foundation of American grand strategy, which is ultimately designed to maintain civil liberty and order in America.

The Means of American Grand Strategy

The Constitution also effectively balanced and controlled the *means* of American grand strategy—the diplomatic, informational, military and economic instruments of

---

[4] Walter A. McDougall, *The Constitutional History of U.S. Foreign Policy: 222 Tears of Tension in the Twilight Zone,* Center for the Study of America and the West, Foreign Policy Research Institute, September 2010, 8.

power. The government was empowered to protect the nation from foreign powers, but constrained to prevent those same powers from oppressing liberty at home. The founding documents themselves—the Declaration of Independence and the Constitution of the United States—and the powerful ideals and principles represent the *informational* instrument of power to guide and empower American grand strategy. The *economic* instrument of power was granted exclusively to Congress, demonstrating the legislative supremacy of the U.S. government. The Constitution also carefully separated, balanced, and checked the primary *means* of foreign policy—the *diplomatic* and *military* instruments of power—between the Executive and Legislative branches.

The *diplomatic instrument of power* is defined in Article II, Section 2 of the Constitution, which states that the President appoints Ambassadors and makes treaties, with the two thirds consent of the present members of the Senate. Treaties are the mechanisms for international relations and one of the most powerful instruments of foreign policy. The shared role in the Constitution for both the President and the Senate in negotiating and ratifying treaties demonstrates the premise of both a separation and a check of power. The reason for the checks on the "treaty-making power of the executive" is explained in *The Federalist Papers*. "The history of human conduct does not warrant that exalted opinion of human virtue which would make it wise in a nation to commit interests of so delicate and momentous a kind, as those which concern its intercourse with the rest of the world, to the sole disposal of a President of the United States."[5] Therefore, the requirement of both the President and the Senate to ratify all

_____

[5] Alexander Hamilton, James Madison, and John Jay, *The Federalist Papers*, ed. Clint Rossiter, (New York: New American Library, 2003), 448-50.

treaties ensured that the "people of America would have greater security against an improper use of the power of making treaties."[6]

The source of the *informational instrument of power* flows from the American Bill of Rights, particularly the right to the freedom of religion, speech, press, and assembly, which demonstrates the power of liberty in the U.S. government. Joint Pub-1 defines the informational instrument of power as: "Information readily available from multiple sources that influences domestic and foreign audiences including citizens, adversaries, and governments."[7] The American way of life and the example of national domestic and foreign policy certainly shape public opinion and national legitimacy around the globe. The founding documents themselves—The Declaration of Independence and the U.S. Constitution—exert tremendous foreign and domestic influence as informational instruments of power in American grand strategy.

The *military instrument of power* is defined largely in Article 1, Section 8: "Congress shall have the Power To…provide for the common Defense." Congress is granted the authority to: 1) raise, support, provide and maintain the military through the power of the purse; 2) make rules to govern and regulate the military; and 3) "declare War, grant Letters of Marque and Reprisal, and make rules concerning Captures on Land and Water." *The Federalist Papers* explain that these powers are not constrained in the Constitution "because it is impossible to foresee or to define the extent and variety of the means which may be necessary to satisfy them."[8] Congress is granted the necessary power to fund, raise and support sufficient military means to provide for the common

---

[6] Ibid., 452.

[7] U.S. Joint Chiefs of Staff. *Doctrine for the Armed Forces of the United States,* Joint Publication 1 (Washington DC: Joint Chiefs of Staff), May 02, 2007, Incorporating Change 1, March 20, 2009, I-9.

[8] Hamilton, Madison, and Jay, 149.

defense against all contingencies—sufficient *means* to effectively respond to a volatile and complex *strategic environment* with *flexibility* and *adaptability*. This provision "rests upon axioms as simple as they are universal; the *means* ought to be proportioned to the *end*; the persons from whose agency the attainment of any *end* is expected ought to possess the *means* by which it is to be attained."[9] Congress was specifically granted these powers instead of the President in order to protect the nation's liberty, even though the President was rightly granted the authority as Commander in Chief. The President has influence, but no authority over the *means* of common defense, because of the fear that this power would be used to build up the military to take control of the government and oppress the people. This design was intended to prevent the United States from repeating the mistakes of the Roman Republic, where the "liberties of Rome proved the final victim to her military triumphs."[10] However, in accordance with Article II, Section 2, the President is the "Commander in Chief" of the military. Once war is declared, the "direction of war…demands…the exercise of power by a single hand…the executive authority"—unity of command.[11] Therefore, once committed to war or military action by the Congress, the President directs the nation's military, which Congress has raised, funded, and maintained.

The *economic instrument of power* is defined in Article 1, Section 8, which states that Congress has been granted the "Power to lay and collect Taxes, Duties, Imposts and Excises, to pay the Debts, and provide for the common Defence and General Welfare of the United States." It has also been granted the following authorities: 1) "To borrow

---

[9] Ibid.

[10] Ibid., 253.

[11] Ibid., 149.

Money on the credit of the United States"; 2) "To regulate Commerce with foreign Nations, among the States and with the Indian Tribes"; and 3) "To coin Money." The economic instrument of power funds all other *means*, which means it determines and drives the overall power of the nation. Therefore, it is the most critical of the instruments of power. Congress has been granted sole authority and power over the national economic instrument of power. This is in keeping with the American tradition of the legislative supremacy of government. It is the ultimate check and balance that the legislative branch has on the other two branches of government.

The Ways of American Grand Strategy

The Constitution addresses strategic ways only generically through the establishment of governing institutions and the limited powers and authorities established for each part. It established three separate and distinct branches of government— Legislative, Executive and Judicial—along with the powers and responsibilities of each. Government officials relied on thorough knowledge of government operations, Constitutional design, international relations and extensive practical self-government experience in maintaining civil liberty and order. Alexis de Tocqueville in his 1835 book, *Democracy in America,* explained that "though the most complete of all known federal constitutions, it is frightening to note how many differences of knowledge and discernment it assumes in those governed....Once the general theory is well understood, the difficulties of applying remain....and it can only suit a nation long accustomed to self-government and where political science reaches right down to the lowest rungs of society."[12]

In the context of foreign policy, the U.S. Constitution provides the means, but relies on successive administrations to determine the ways through foreign policy traditions to govern and guide international relations. The Constitution is very clear on the powers, authorities and responsibilities of the government to develop foreign policy and international relations. These means include the appointment of ambassadors, ratification of treaties, the provision, regulation and use of the military, and the declaration of war. However, there is no specific guidance on specific ways to execute American foreign policy in pursuit of national interests.[13] Foreign policy was to be designed by the elected officials that would serve in the federal government as accountable representatives of the people. The design of the constitutional government provided the elected officials the institutional means to exercise their collective wisdom and judgment to discern "how" to promote and secure national interests effectively in a volatile and complex strategic environment with flexibility and adaptability. Each successive Presidential administrations developed foreign policies. Some of these foreign policies are broadly accepted as traditions. These traditions defined the ways of American grand strategy. The remainder of this section will examine and criticize the effectiveness of these foreign policy traditions.

---

[12] Alexis De Tocqueville, *Democracy in America,* trans. Gerald E. Bevan (London: Penguin Books Ltd., 1971), 193.

[13] McDougall, *The Constitutional History of U.S. Foreign Policy,* 8.

American Foreign Policy Traditions

American foreign policy traditions formed the basic building blocks for international relations, which supported and complemented the U.S. Constitution in the historical continuum of American grand strategy. Walter McDougall identified eight American *traditions* that shaped and guided the continuum of American foreign policy. These traditions all possessed the same enduring characteristics in that they "commanded solid bipartisan support, outlived the era that gave it birth, entered the permanent lexicon of our national discourse, and continued to resonate with a portion of the American public even during eras when it did not directly inspire policy."[14] The first four foundational foreign policy traditions—Liberty/Exceptionalism, Unilateralism, The American System, and Expansionism—were established by the Founding Fathers during their Presidential administrations, which included George Washington, John Adams, Thomas Jefferson, James Madison and James Monroe. The second four traditions—Progressive Imperialism, Wilsonianism/Liberal Internationalism, Containment, and Global Meliorism—departed in varying degrees from the foundational foreign policy traditions that defined American grand strategy during the first century of the United States. These traditions were established after 1898, during a period of tremendous change in the strategic environment. However, these new traditions involved more than just responses to a change in the strategic environment. They challenged America's traditional identity and role in the world, as well as the fundamental assumption of the unchanging character of human nature.

---

[14] McDougall, *Promised Land, Crusader State,* 10.

America's Foundational Foreign Policy Traditions

Liberty (Exceptionalism)

The central idea of American Liberty was that the United States was by nature exceptional, as enshrined in the Declaration of Independence and the U.S. Constitution. As has been discussed at length, America was unique and special, but that Exceptionalism did not include or justify a universal mission to Americanize the world. The prevailing national identity was to limit the expression of American Exceptionalism to "Liberty at home" versus a revolutionary nation on a universal militant crusade to proselytize the world with America's religion or democratic form of government.[15] Alexander Hamilton alludes to this aversion to a revolutionary foreign policy in the first article of *The Federalist Papers*: "For in politics, as in religion, it is equally absurd to aim at making proselytes by fire and sword. Heresies in either can rarely be cured by persecution."[16] The "exceptional calling of the American people was not *to do* anything special in foreign affairs, but *to be* a light"—a beacon of liberty and order.[17] The early American administrations, demonstrating their collective will in a "remarkable display of unanimity and good judgment, agreed to limit the content of American Exceptionalism to Liberty at home, period."[18]

The French Revolution was a difficult challenge to the young republic's resolve to separate themselves from European conflict by remaining neutral, because of their passionate support for liberty. Despite passionate public support, America maintained strict neutrality throughout the French Revolution and the subsequent war between

---

[15] Ibid., 21.

[16] Hamilton, Madison, and Jay, 29.

[17] McDougall, *Promised Land, Crusader State*, 20-21.

[18] Ibid.

France and Great Britain. According to historian Joyce Appleby, the French Revolution and European war "succeeded in bringing to the surface of public life opposing conceptions of society."[19] This caused resurgence of the "aristocratic-versus-popular clash" resurfacing the great debate concerning the "fundamental questions about human nature and social norms" as it applied to America.[20] The Federalist's pro-British stance was interpreted as "favor for a hierarchical society *at home*;" whereas, the Democratic Republicans' pro-French stance was interpreted as "favor for extreme democracy *at home*."[21] However, there was little support for war to support France. The anarchy and chaos resulting from the French Revolution was brutal and bloody evidence of the reality of human nature and the danger of extreme and unchecked popular democracy, which confirmed the wisdom of the Constitution. This also confirmed the foreign policy wisdom of *neutrality* versus support or intervention in revolutionary wars.

Wisely, the "Americans resisted the intense ideological and military pressure put on them in the 1790s to succumb to the temptation to turn their foreign policy into a crusade."[22] For the Founding Fathers, political innovations and institutions were an "end in itself"—to secure American liberty—and not to channel foreign policy in militant crusades to promote the spread of liberty.[23] Though crusades were not acceptable, the young republic still required military power to "provide for the common defence" as required in the Preamble of the Constitution. America's liberty required a strong defense,

---

[19] Ibid., 30.

[20] Joyce Appleby, *Capitalism and a New Social Order: The Republican Vision of the 1790s* (New York: New York University Press, 1984), 58.

[21] McDougall, *Promised Land, Crusader State*, 20.

[22] Ibid., 32.

[23] Ibid., 20.

which demanded military power. However, America used military power in the world only to defend their liberty in accordance with their grand strategy. The United States defended her liberty and independence both in international waters and at home in the Barbary Wars and the War of 1812. The United States refused to get embroiled in the Latin American wars of independence against Spain, but did use the opportunity to codify America's traditional foreign policy in the context of American Liberty/Exceptionalism.

In 1821, congressional representatives pressured President Monroe to assist Latin American juntas in their fight for independence from Spain. John Quincy Adams, Monroe's Secretary of State refuted the "heretical doctrine of a crusader America" and articulated the "orthodox dogma of American Exceptionalism" in his Fourth of July address.[24]

> America, in the assembly of nations, since her admission among them, has invariably, though often fruitlessly, held forth to them the hand of honest friendship, of equal freedom, of generous reciprocity….She has in the lapse of *nearly a half a century*, without a single exception, respected the independence of other nations, while asserting and maintaining her own. She has abstained from interference in the concerns of others, even when the conflict has been for the principles to which she clings, as to the last vital drop that visits the heart….But she *does not go abroad in search of monsters to destroy.* She is the *well-wisher to the freedom and independence of all.* She is the *champion only of her own.* She will recommend the general cause by the countenance of her voice, and the benignant sympathy of her example.[25]

Adams refers to the unbroken continuity of foreign policy since 1776, which is testimony to the continuum of American grand strategy during the Presidential administrations of

---

[24] Ibid., 36.

[25] John Quincy Adams, "An address, delivered at the request of the committee of arrangements for celebrating the Anniversary of Independence, at the city of Washington on the fourth Of July 1821 by John Quincy Adams," 31-32, A Collection of Fourth of July Speeches from the Special Collections of Ellis Library, University of Missouri-Columbia, http://digital.library.umsystem.edu/cgi/t/text/text-idx?sid=508ff392ee876697f6ad60d6f09e4dc3;g=;c=jul;idno=jul000088 (accessed, March 1, 2012).

the Founding Fathers from Washington to Monroe. America's foreign policy was characterized by a zealous defense of her own freedom, but not a trace of foreign adventures or crusades "abroad in search of monsters to destroy."

America did not "champion" or fight for the "freedom and independence of all." Why? Adams answers unequivocally.

> She well knows that by once enlisting under other banners of foreign independence, she would involve herself beyond the power of extrication, in all the wars of interest and intrigue, of individual avarice, envy, and ambition, which assumed the colors and usurped the standards of freedom....The fundamental maxims of her policy would insensibly change from *liberty* to *force*....She might become the dictatress of the world. She would be no longer the ruler of her own spirit.[26]

Wars of independence require *force* to impose foreign policy. Therefore, America would be fighting an endless series of protracted wars to champion liberty other than her own. America's foreign policy would become one of military force, instead of the traditional policy of liberty, which allowed each nation to shape its own destiny. Therefore, each nation has the responsibility to fight their own battles in the cause for freedom and liberty. A nation must fight for her own freedom if she is to be worthy of it and capable of keeping it. The very act of organizing and unifying to fight forges a national community—a people.

The American government established by the Constitution provided sufficient *means* to "provide for the common defence" of American Liberty. As the 'champion only of her own liberty', America's own experiences had proven the "timeless wisdom of the Roman motto—If you desire peace, prepare for war." However, war was to defend

---

[26] Ibid.

liberty at home. The warning is clear; "idealistic or revolutionary foreign policy," which led to fighting wars as foreign crusades for independence and liberty, would sacrifice America's liberty in the process. Therefore, the means of foreign policy and military power were not instruments of power to spread liberty to the world but as instruments for protection, preservation, and expansion of America's exceptional liberty in America.[27] Thus, American Liberty and Exceptionalism served the United States well during the first century of the nation's history and coupled seamlessly with the traditional foreign policy of Unilateralism.

Unilateralism

Unilateralism interlocked with American Liberty, because unilateralism avoided the entangling alliances that would have drawn the U.S. needlessly into European wars counter to vital national interests. Internationalists discount the American tradition of *Unilateralism* as a disguised form of isolationism, instead of a legitimate foreign policy tradition. However, Washington and Jefferson stood firm in their principles of unilateralism for the United States of America since "entangling alliances would impinge on U.S. sovereignty, harm its interests, or restrict its freedom of action."[28] American Unilateralism was "to be *at Liberty*" to freely choose the nation's foreign policy based on vital national interests independent of the European powers.[29] Therefore, "*neutrality* was the only moral *and* pragmatic course for the new nation."[30]

---

[27] McDougall, *Promised Land, Crusader State*, 218.

[28] Ibid., 217.

[29] Ibid., 40.

[30] Ibid., 42.

President George Washington's 1796 Farewell Address defined the "The Great

Rule" of foreign policy for the next century:

> The *great rule of conduct for us in regard to foreign nations* is in *extending our commercial relations*, to have with them *as little political connection as possible*….Our *detached and distant situation* invites and enables us to pursue a different course. If we remain one people under an efficient government, the period is not far off when we may defy material injury from external annoyance; when we may take such an attitude as will cause the *neutrality we may at any time resolve upon to be scrupulously respected*; when belligerent nations, under the impossibility of making acquisitions upon us, will not lightly hazard the giving us provocation; when *we may choose peace or war, as our interest, guided by justice, shall counsel.*[31]

George Washington also extended his great rule of unilateralism to commercial

trade, because treating all trading partners fairly and equally ultimately provided the most

effective means for healthier long-term international trade relationships.

> Observe good faith and justice towards all nations; cultivate peace and harmony with all….Harmony, liberal intercourse with all nations, are recommended by policy, humanity, and interest. But even our *commercial policy should hold an equal and impartial hand*; neither seeking nor granting exclusive favors or preferences; consulting the natural course of things; diffusing and diversifying by gentle means the streams of commerce, but forcing nothing….There can be *no greater error than to expect or calculate upon real favors from nation to nation*. It is *an illusion, which experience must cure*, which a just pride ought to discard.[32]

Neutrality without the entanglements of alliances or binding treaties enabled the

United States to act according to vital national interests in keeping with American values.

However, Washington also understood that avoiding all alliances was unrealistic for the

United States. Therefore, he provided some balancing principles. "It is our true policy to

steer clear of *permanent alliances* with any portion of the foreign world; so far, I mean,

---

[31] George Washington, "George Washington's Farewell Address, 1796," Avalon Project: Documents in Law, History and Diplomacy, Lillian Goldman Law Library, Yale Law School, http://avalon.law.yale.edu/18th_century/washing.asp (accessed September 20, 2011).

[32] Ibid.

as we are now at liberty to do it....Taking care always to keep ourselves by suitable establishments on a *respectable defensive posture*, we may safely trust to *temporary alliances for extraordinary emergencies*."[33] The need for defensive military strength became essential to America's grand strategy, because a "respectable defense posture" was the key to remain neutral and free of European entanglements.

In American grand strategy, a unilateral foreign policy and respectable military power served to protect the nation's liberty at home and enforce her neutral rights abroad. Alexis de Tocqueville expounded on the military's role in economic growth and diplomatic respect: "Reason suggests and experience proves that no commercial greatness can last unless it is linked to a military power whenever the need arises. The truth of this is as fully understood in the United States as everywhere else. The Americans are already able to inspire respect for their flag; soon they will be able to make it feared."[34]

America had to enforce neutral rights with military power. Neutrality alone did not protect the United States from violations of their international rights at sea. The United States funded and fielded a stronger military and used their fledgling naval power and Marines—instead of the customary tribute—to secure American shipping in the Mediterranean from Tripoli pirates in the Barbary Wars. However, Great Britain and France provided the greatest challenge to the United States. Both the British and the French violated American neutrality during their war with each other. Each nation captured American merchant ships and seized their cargos to disrupt the flow of trade to

---

[33] Ibid.

[34] Alexis De Tocqueville, *Democracy in America,* trans. by Gerald E. Bevan (London: Penguin Books Ltd., 1971), 478.

their enemy. Despite strict neutrality, the "Atlantic Ocean came alive with enemies of

American trade" and the United States had to respond to the volatile change in the

strategic environment.[35] France "captured more than three hundred American ships in

the first year alone," and suggested that the Americans pay tribute for safe passage.

Americans united in a common cry for "Millions for defense, but not one cent for

tribute!"[36] Congress responded by raising an army and establishing the Navy Department

to enforce the freedom of the seas with capital ships. American naval power finally

drove France to ratify the Treaty of Mortefontaine in 1800, which officially ended the

French-American alliance brokered during the Revolutionary War and formally

established the European neutrality of the United States. However, American neutrality

did not mean isolation from Europe.

Neutrality, as the Founding Fathers understood it, was "the perfect independence

of the United States; not their isolation from the great affairs of the world."[37] Isolation

was impossible, since the United States depended largely on Europe for trade and Great

Britain remained the nation's primary trading partner. The 1795 British (Jay) Treaty

facilitated a workable trade relationship with Britain for a decade before relations

deteriorated during Britain's war with France. Eventually, the dispute over freedom of

the seas led to the War of 1812 with the British, which many considered the "second

struggle for our liberty."[38] President James Madison tried to avoid war but did not shrink

from war because he "acknowledged that on the element which forms three-fourths of the

---

[35] McDougall, *Promised Land, Crusader State,* 33.

[36] Ibid., 31.

[37] Ibid., 50.

[38] Ibid., 35.

globe we inhabit, and where all independent nations have equal and common rights, the Americans were not an independent people, but colonists and vassals."[39] Despite the British advantage, America fought the War of 1812 unilaterally without an alliance with France to defend American neutral rights of the sea. The war did little to change the status quo, but it gained the United States a measure of respect from the European powers

Ultimately, Washington's wisdom and judgment set a firm foundation for an effective grand strategy in a very dangerous strategic environment. The "Great Rule"— American Unilateralism—continued to guide foreign policy in every subsequent administration for the rest of the century by maintaining neutrality and avoiding permanent foreign entanglements or alliances.[40] Unilateralism protected America from the politics and wars of Europe through neutrality. However, the Monroe Doctrine took it one step further and called for neutral reciprocity from Europe in order to establish the American System on the continent.

The American System (Monroe Doctrine)

The Monroe Doctrine was an American unilateral declaration "as a principle in which the rights and interests of the United States are involved that the American continents, by the free and independent condition which they have assumed and maintain, are henceforth not to be considered as subjects for future colonization by any European powers."[41] The War of 1812 had established the United States as a significant power on

---

[39] James Madison, "State of the Union, Fourth Annual Message, November 4, 1812", The American Presidency Project, University of California, Santa Barbara, http://www.presidency.ucsb.edu/ws/index.php?pid=29454#axzz1vvebVci6 (accessed September 20, 2011).

[40] McDougall, *Promised Land, Crusader State,*, 49.

[41] James Monroe, "Monroe Doctrine: President Monroe's seventh annual message to Congress, December 2, 1823." Avalon Project: Documents in Law, History and Diplomacy. Lillian Goldman Law Library, Yale Law School. http://avalon.law.yale.edu/19th_century/monroe.asp (accessed September 12,

the American continent, capable of defending their nation and interests effectively.

Despite this defensive capability, the United States did not have a large enough navy to

challenge an imperial power directly.[42] However, America harbored no interests or intent

to "provide moral or material support to revolutionary movements in Europe" or Latin

America.[43] In that context, President Monroe further declared:

> In the wars of the European powers in matters relating to themselves we
> have never taken any part, nor does it comport with our policy to do so. It
> is only when our rights are invaded or seriously menaced that we resent
> injuries or make preparation for our defense. With the movements in this
> hemisphere we are of necessity more immediately connected, and by
> causes which must be obvious to all enlightened and impartial observers.
> The political system of the allied powers is essentially different in this
> respect from that of America....We owe it, therefore, to candor and to the
> amicable relations existing between the United States and those powers to
> declare that we should consider any attempt on their part to extend their
> system to any portion of this hemisphere as dangerous to our peace and
> safety.[44]

President Monroe was warning Europe that it was a vital U.S. national interest to prevent

any European powers from interfering with or imposing their political system on the

Western Hemisphere in order to preserve American Liberty.[45]

President Monroe also declared the intentions and expectations of the United

States concerning European colonies in the Western Hemisphere, particularly the Latin

American colonies that had declared their independence from Spain. The United States

---

2011). "Our policy in regard to Europe, which was adopted at an early stage of the wars which have so
long agitated that quarter of the globe, nevertheless remains the same, which is, not to interfere in the
internal concerns of any of its powers; to consider the government de facto as the legitimate
government for us; to cultivate friendly relations with it, and to preserve those relations by a frank,
firm, and manly policy, meeting in all instances the just claims of every power, submitting to injuries
from none."

[42] McDougall, *Promised Land, Crusader State*, 73.

[43] Ibid., 75.

[44] Monroe.

[45] McDougall, *Promised Land, Crusader State*, 74.

maintained strict neutrality during the Latin American revolutions from Spanish control, and did not intervene or assist.[46] President Monroe knew that if the United States was challenged directly by an imperial power, the Monroe Doctrine would have been virtually impossible to enforce. Nonetheless, he declared it as a unilateral statement of intent that expected reciprocity from the imperial powers, based on America's proven record of neutrality and non-interference.[47]

> With the existing colonies or dependencies of any European power we have not interfered and shall not interfere. But with the Governments who have declared their independence and maintain it, and whose independence we have, on great consideration and on just principles, acknowledged, we could not view any interposition for the purpose of oppressing them, or controlling in any other manner their destiny, by any European power in any other light than as the manifestation of an unfriendly disposition toward the United States….It is still the true policy of the United States to leave the parties to themselves, in hope that other powers will pursue the same course.[48]

The Monroe Doctrine was intended to persuade Spain and the European Allies to disengage from the continent in order to gain Florida and give the Latin American Colonies the best chance for independence. However, the Monroe Doctrine was not intended to unite North and South America in common cause or in one community. Secretary of State John Quincy Adams did not support American intervention or assistance to the Latin American countries because he reasoned that "if they cannot beat Spain, they do not deserve to be free."[49] As far as Adams was concerned, the American system did not include Latin America, because they were not part of the American community. "As to an *American system*, we have it; we constitute the whole of it; there

---

[46] Ibid., 66-7.

[47] Ibid., 73.

[48] Monroe.

[49] McDougall, *Promised Land, Crusader State*, 68.

is no community of interests or of principles between North and South America."[50]

Therefore, there was no common culture or common interests, values or rights to justify a merging of the North and South American communities. Adams explained his reasoning in his memoirs:

> That the final issue of their present struggle would be their entire independence of Spain I had never doubted. That it was our true policy and duty to take no part in the contest I was equally clear. The *principle of neutrality* to *all* foreign wars is, in my opinion, fundamental to the continuance of our liberties and of our Union. So far as they were contending for independence, I wished well to their cause; but I had seen and yet see no prospect that they would establish free or liberal institutions of government. They are not likely to promote the spirit either of *freedom* or *order* by their example....We should derive no improvement to our own institutions by any communion with theirs. Nor was there any appearance of a disposition in them to take any political lesson from us.[51]

Ultimately, the Monroe Doctrine was an effective, inexpensive and sustainable foreign policy component of grand strategy that established an American System, and safeguarded the nation's Liberty. In fact, it was America's neutrality and integrity in international relations—coupled with their fierce defense of vital national interests—that won the nation a measure of respect and autonomy on the American continent well beyond her military power to command that respect. The grand strategy could be summarized as the "Monroe Doctrine and the Golden Rule," which encouraged

---

[50] John Quincy Adams, *Memoirs of John Quincy Adams, Comprising Portions of His Diary from 1795 to 1848*. ed. Charles Francis Adams (Philadelphia: J. B. Lippincott & Co., 1875), 176, University of California Digital Library, http://www.archive.org/details/memjohnquinc05adamrich (accessed March 1, 2012). Adams explained further: "They have not the first elements of good or free government. Arbitrary power, military and ecclesiastical, was stamped upon their education, upon their habits, and upon all their institutions. Civil dissension was infused into all their seminal principles. War and mutual destruction was in every member of their organization, moral, political, and physical. I had little expectation of any beneficial result to this country from any future connection with them, political or commercial."

[51] Ibid, 324-5.

reciprocity and fair dealings based on national interests.[52]   Ultimately, the Monroe

Doctrine was effective because the "Continental powers accepted Anglo-American

domination of the western hemisphere, and preferred to fence Europe off from the

quarrels, troubles, and dangerous ideologies of North and South America."[53]   Though the

Latin Americans did win their independence, it is critical to note that the United States

refused to embark on a militant crusade against the imperial tyranny of Spain to support

the revolutions.   However, conflicting interests between independent North and South

America would eventually lead to war with Mexico as America expanded west toward

the Pacific Ocean in the tradition of American Expansionism.

Expansionism

American Expansionism was expressed by expansive purchases and annexations

of land by the American government, as well as the passion and capability of the

American people to conquer and populate the new lands.   In fact, the early history of the

United States represents the expansive growth to populate the continental limits of North

America.   Expansionism was a major expression of American growth and the need to

expand because "Geography invited it; demography compelled it."[54]   Expansion also

gave Americans a sense of purpose for their labors.   A nation of farmers moved west to

populate and harvest the abundant fruits of an expanding frontier.   Inventors and

manufacturers used innovative technologies and infrastructure improvements—"canals,

levees, steamboats, clipper ships, steam-assisted ships, turnpikes, the telegraph,

railroads"—to conquer an expansive land and harness its vast natural resources.

---

[52] McDougall, *Promised Land, Crusader State*, 57.

[53] Ibid., 73.

[54] Ibid., 79.

Merchants expanded trade to open new markets for the bountiful raw materials and manufactured goods, as well as, meet the growing demand for imported goods.[55]

Expansionism was an inseparable extension of the unilateral American System of Liberty/Exceptionalism. Thomas Jefferson believed that "our rapid multiplication will…cover the whole northern if not southern continent, with people speaking the same language, governed by similar forms, and by similar laws."[56] Therefore, he believed that America would expand naturally in an American System of like-minded communities that would be seamlessly federated into the United States in accordance with the Constitution and long-standing tradition. Though John Quincy Adams did not include the southern continent in the American System, he had similar visions for continental expansion: "North America appears to be destined by Divine Providence to be peopled by one *nation*, speaking one language, professing one general system of religious and political principles, and accustomed to one general tenor of social usages and customs. For the common happiness of them all, for their peace and prosperity, I believe it is indispensable that they should be associated with one federal Union."[57] The critical point to these visions of American Expansionism is not the physical expansion that naturally accompanies the growth of a national population, but rather the harmonious Union of the expanding frontier as a seamless extension of the United States. These visions did not include the annexation of foreign lands, densely populated by people that spoke a different language, professed a different religion and governed by different political

---

[55] Ibid., 79-80.

[56] Ibid., 78.

[57] John Quincy Adams, *The Writings of John Quincy Adams,1811-1813,* vol. IV, ed. by Worthington Chauncey Ford, (New York: MacMillan Company, 1914), 209, University of California Digital Library, http://archive.org/details/fordsjohnadams04adamrich (accessed 25 May 2012).

principles. These visions were entirely consistent with the American context of community. There was no interest in disrupting the harmonious union of communities professing the same interests, rights and values. American Liberty was to be the centerpiece of community and unity throughout the continent, without any foreign influence or interference. Thus, there was no interest in accommodating or integrating foreign cultures or colonies in the process. In fact, the footholds of potential imperial power on the continent—such as British control of Oregon or California—represented a threat to American Liberty.[58] Therefore, *Expansionism* sought to expand the *American System* of *Liberty* on the continent *unilaterally*.

However, popular religious movements created a more idealistic religious interpretation of the traditional vision of Expansionism—"Manifest Destiny"—served as a strong competing ideological undercurrent.[59] Due to the religious foundation of America, Robert Fogel argues that the "process of political change…is to a large extent spawned by trends in American religiosity."[60] Examples of this include the political anti-slavery and temperance movements that sprang out of the Second Great Awakenings from 1840 to 1870.[61] There was still a clear separation between the church and the state. However, in a government empowered by the people via popular sovereignty, large popular movements, including religious ones, greatly influenced and shaped the politics and policy of the nation. According to Timothy Smith, "The civil religion of the

---

[58] McDougall, *Promised Land, Crusader State*, 77-8.

[59] Ibid., 84.

[60] Robert Fogel, "The Fourth Great Awakening and the Political Realignment of the 1990s", American Enterprise Institute for Public Policy Research, AEI Bradley Lecture Series, September 11, 1995, http://www.aei.org/speech/society-and-culture/religion/the-fourth-great-awakening-and-the-political-realignment-of-the-1990s, (accessed May 25, 2012).

[61] Ibid.

American people thus came to rest not on the faith the Enlightenment had awakened in man's moral powers…but on revivalistic, reform-minded, and millennial Christianity."[62] Western revivals collectively fostered a growing belief that God had "reconsecrated America the New Israel and ascribed to it the power to inaugurate Christ's thousand-year reign on earth."[63] These radical beliefs fueled the progressive, and more aggressively expansionist political movement commonly referred to as Manifest Destiny.

John O'Sullivan, the editor of *Democratic Review*, which supported and promoted Jacksonian democracy, coined the term "Manifest Destiny," which articulated a growing popular movement towards progressive ideology in America. He passionately argued that American expansion was justified because the claim on the land s were by the "right of our manifest destiny to overspread and to possess the whole continent which Providence has given us for the development of the great experiment of Liberty and federated self-government entrusted to us," which sparked heated debate in Congress.[64] Of course, this supposedly incontestable right to the continent was at the expense of the original inhabitants of the North American continent—the American Indians, but this ugly reality was rarely considered. According to historian Julius Pratt, Manifest Destiny became rooted in the American identity because "Before the Oregon question was settled,

---

[62] Timothy L. Smith, "Righteousness and Hope: Christian Holiness and the Millenial Vision in America, 1880-1900," American Quarterly 31, no. 1 (Spring 1979): 38-39, http://www.jstor.org/discover/10.2307/2712485?uid=3739936&uid=2129&uid=2&uid=70&uid=4&uid=3739256&sid=47699037800717, (accessed May 25, 2012).

[63] McDougall, *Promised Land, Crusader State*, 81.

[64] New York Morning News editorial, "The True Title," December 27, 1845, attributed to John L. O'Sullivan, editor of the monthly *Democratic Review* and the New York *Morning News*, quoted in Julius W. Pratt, "The Origin of 'Manifest Destiny'," *The American Historical Review* 32, no. 4 (July 1927): 795-798, http://www.jstor.org/stable/1837859 (accessed 25 May 2012). Though the article referred directly to the debate on which nation owned the title to Oregon, Manifest Destiny became the radical justification for continental American Expansionism. O'Sullivan went further to state: "The God of nature and of nations has marked it [the continent] for our own; and with His blessing we will firmly maintain the *incontestable* rights He has given, and fearlessly perform the high duties He has imposed."

the nation was engaged in the war with Mexico, and the enthusiasm for expansion at the

expense of our southern neighbor served to popularize and perpetuate the phrase."[65]

The ideology of Manifest Destiny modified American Exceptionalism by

universalizing the politics and religion of the American experience as the true path for

universal *human progress*. For instance, O'Sullivan's *Democratic Review* propagated

this popular viewpoint: "Democracy in its true sense is the last best revelation of human

thought. We speak, of course, of that true and genuine Democracy which breathes the air

and lives in the light of Christianity—whose essence is justice, and whose object is

human progress."[66] Of course, this did not include progress or justice for the American

Indians or the African slaves. In the case of the Indians, Alexis de Tocqueville observed

in the 1830s that Americans "have been unable to alter entirely the Indian character and,

although they have the power to destroy them, they do not possess the power to civilize

or to reduce them to submission."[67] Therefore, Manifest Destiny was supposed to be

"peaceful, automatic, gradual, and governed by self-determination"—in accordance with

---

[65] Julius W. Pratt, "The Origin of 'Manifest Destiny'," *The American Historical Review* 32, no. 4 (July 1927): 795-798, http://www.jstor.org/stable/1837859 (accessed 25 May 2012).

[66] John L. O'Sullivan, "Democracy," *The United States Democratic Review* 7, Issue 27 (March 1840): 215-229, American Memory: The Nineteenth Century in Print: Periodicals, http://memory.loc.gov/cgi-bin/query/r?ammem/ncps:@field(DOCID+@lit(AGD1642-0007-18)) (accessed May 25, 2012). "Democracy must finally triumph in human reason, because its foundations are deep in the human heart.... We have nosympathy with much that usurps the name, like that fierce and turbulent spirit of ancient Greece which was only the monstrous misgrowth of faction and fraud, or that Democracy whose only distinction is the slave-like observance of party usages—the dumb repetition of party creeds; and still less for that wild, reckless spirit of mobism which triumphs, with remorseless and fiendish exultation, over all lawful authority, all constituted restraint. The object of our worship [democracy] is far different from these; the present offering is made to a spirit which asserts a virtuous freedom of act and thought which insists on the rights of men, demands the equal diffusion of every social advantage, asks the impartial participation of every gift of God, sympathizes with the down-trodden, rejoices in their elevationand proclaims to the world the sovereignty not of the people barely, but of immutable justice and truth....Democracy must finally reign."

[67] Alexis de Tocqueville, *Democracy in America,* trans. by Gerald E. Bevan (London: Penguin Books Ltd., 1971), 373. An example includes the Indian Removal Act of 1830. Tocqueville includes an entire section entitled "The Three Races in the United States" that addresses the challenges and contradictions in America concerning the American Indians and the African slaves.

the principles of civil liberty and popular sovereignty—but the reality contradicted the intent and policies of the Founding Fathers due to the racial discrimination and militant means used to resolve the conflict with the American Indians.[68] Regardless of these glaring contradictions of human progress, the United States marched onward with expansionism to realize the continental dream of Manifest Destiny.

In order for the United States to realize her Manifest Destiny, President Polk initiated his western Expansionist agenda in his First Annual Message of 1845 by applying the Monroe Doctrine to the annexation of new states.

> We must ever maintain the principle that the people of this continent alone have the right to decide their own destiny. Should any portion of them, constituting an independent state, propose to unite themselves with our Confederacy, this will be a question for them and us to determine without any foreign interposition…. In the existing circumstances of the world the present is deemed a proper occasion to reiterate and reaffirm the principle avowed by Mr. Monroe and to state my cordial concurrence in its wisdom and sound policy…and that it should be distinctly announced to the world as our settled policy that no future European colony or dominion shall

---

[68] McDougall, *Promised Land, Crusader State*, 86-90. "The real moral quandary posed by expansion arose from the conflict between American liberty, which enabled and justified national expansion, and the fact that expansion occurred at the expense of dispossessed Indians, Mexicans, and (to the extent slavery spread) Africa." "Enlightenment philosophy taught the unity of mankind and the concept of the noble savage," which gave hope tha the Indians would "gradually take their place as individuals within the dominant culture." Washington and Jefferson focused on education and a "humane program based on restriction of white settlement, recognition of Indian lands [The Northwest Ordinance], funding of religious and agricultural missions, regulation of trade with the Indians, and the conclusion of treaties with tribes as if they were foreign nations." However, the policies of mutual respect and assimilation failed due to the inevitable reality of land encroachment, the tribal desire to preserve Indian culture, competition between state governments and tribal authorities, and the inevitable conflict—often resulting in primordial violence—between Americans and Indian Tribes. "Whereas Christian and Enlightenment doctrines preached human uniformity and the prevalence of nurture over nature, the first evolutionary theories…suggested the prevalence of nature over nurture…the hypothesis of biological inequality." "That Americans used racial arguments to *justify* their claim to eminent domain over whatever lands they fancied is undeniable, but racial aggression was never their *motive* for expansion." Their motives were driven by liberty, opportunity and security, which led to such policies as the Indian Removal Act of 1830 under Jackson. Therefore, racial discrimination—fueled by the "empirical fact" of evolutionary racial superiority—was used to justify the means. "Indians had to be understood as not possessing the rights of citizens" to justify the inhumane policies necessary to continue the expansion of Manifest Destiny.

with our consent be planted or established on any part of the North American continent.[69]

President Polk's perspective on annexation was shaped by the disputed Oregon territory, and the vast, but sparsely populated, Mexican lands—Texas, New Mexico, and California—that stretched west to the Pacific Ocean. Polk admitted that he had "California and the fine bay of San Francisco as much in view as Oregon," but California belonged to Mexico.[70] However, California was the ultimate goal for expansion and the British were interested in securing it for themselves, which would have been unacceptable under the Monroe Doctrine. The U.S. Navy had surveyed the port and reported that: "Upper California may boast one of the finest, if not the very best harbor in the world—that of San Francisco," which was critical to defend the west coast and promote trade in the Pacific.[71] However, Mexico would not sell California to the Americans or any other territory. Instead, Santa Anna broke off diplomatic relations and chose war instead of negotiations.

The Mexican-American War: A Traditional Punitive War

The Mexican-American War is a controversial war, but it serves as an important example of a successful American punitive war in the tradition of the Barbary Wars and the War of 1812. Ultimately, the war achieved America's limited objectives, and

---

[69] James K. Polk, "James K. Polk, First Annual Message, December 2, 1845," ed. by Gerhard Peters and John Woolley, University of California at Santa Barbara, *The American Presidency Project*, http://www.presidency.ucsb.edu/ws/?pid=29486 (accessed May 25, 2012).

[70] James K. Polk, *The Diary of James K. Polk During His Presidency, 1845 to 1849, Vol. 1*, ed. by Milo Milton Quaife (Chicago: A. C. McClurg & Co., 1910), 71, HathiTrust Digital Library, http://hdl.handle.net/2027/loc.ark:/13960/t6d221j44?urlappend=%3Bseq=117 (accessed May 25, 2012).

[71] Charles Wilkes, *United States' Exploring Expedition, During the Years 1838-1842*, (London: Whittaker and Co., 1845), 303, HathiTrust Digital Library, http://hdl.handle.net/2027/uc2.ark:/13960/t59c6th8j (accessed May 25, 2012).

reestablished the security of the nation in accordance with national interests. The Mexican-American War was justified as a defensive war in response to Mexican aggression. However, the war was truly a punitive war to secure national interests and establish a stable peace. The United States executed a *valid* and effective strategy, through a military invasion to conquer Santa Anna's army and occupy Mexico City in order to secure the southern border, as well as acquire the North American territory required for national security and interests. However, the political developments in Mexico that preceded the Mexican-American War provide a relevant case study into the effectiveness of exporting the principles and institutions of the U.S. Constitution to a foreign nation in order to establish a government that promotes civil liberty and order.

In 1824, Mexico established a new constitution, which used the U.S. Constitution as a model. However, this did not establish a stable balance of civil liberty and order within Mexico. There has been a tendency to elevate the U.S. Constitution to mythical status and place too much faith in the power of the document, political theory and the institutions to create civil liberty and order in other countries regardless of preexisting national conditions. The Founding Fathers designed the U.S. Constitution to govern the strong, but united, State-governed local communities of the United States of America. The favorable pre-conditions in America—common core culture and religion favorable to civil liberty, widespread popular consent, a unified people, and effective representative local and state governments—are not a realistic expectation outside America. In his authoritative work, *Democracy in America,* Alexis de Tocqueville concluded that it was unlikely that the U.S. Constitution was exportable because America's federal government "can only suit a nation long accustomed to self-government."[72] Tocqueville used the

instability Mexico experienced after instituting the 1824 Constitution as his case in point.

> The Constitution of the United States is akin to those fine creations of
> human endeavor which crown their inventors with renown and wealth but
> remain sterile in other hands. Contemporary Mexico has illustrated this
> very thing. The Mexicans, aiming for a federal system, took the federal
> constitution of their neighbors, the Anglo-Americans, as their model and
> copied it almost exactly. But although they transported the letter of the
> law, they failed to transfer at the same time the spirit which gave it life.
> As a result, they became tangled endlessly in the machinery of their
> double system of government. The sovereignty of the states and Union
> entered into a collision course as they exceeded the sphere of influence
> assigned to them by the constitution. Even today Mexico veers constantly
> from anarchy to military despotism and back again.[73]

In 1836, Texas declared independence from Mexico as the country veered back

towards military despotism under Santa Anna, who had voided Mexico's 1824

Constitution.[74] The newly independent Republic of Texas requested to be annexed by the

United States in a "clear case of self-determination," since American settlers

outnumbered Mexicans by "seven or eight to one."[75] The divisive issue of slavery in the

new territory delayed the annexation, but Congress finally annexed Texas as a state in

1845.[76]

---

[72] Tocqueville, 193.

[73] Ibid., 194.

[74] Walter A. McDougall, *Promised Land, Crusader State*, 90.

[75]Ibid. "Stephen F. Austin led the first three hundred families across the Sabine River in 1821, promising that they would become Catholics and loyal Mexican citizens." In accordance with the 1821 land grant: "The New Republic of Mexico grants lands in the sparely populated Texas state on the condition settlers convert to Catholicism and assume Mexican citizenship. The Mexicans hoped this would help control raids by Commanches and stop possible expansion into the area by the United States by integrating these new settlers into Mexican society." http://mexicanhistory.org/MexicanAmericanWarTimeline.htm

[76] D. H. Montgomery, *The Leading Facts of American History* (Boston: Ginn & Company, 1903), 262. "By the Missouri Compromise slavery could not be extended west of the Mississippi, outside of Missouri, north of 36° 30' (the southern boundary of Missouri). Unless, therefore, the South got more territory annexed southwest of the Mississippi, the North would soon have the chief power in Congress."

Despite President Polk's efforts to negotiate a settlement of the Rio Grande border dispute and the sale of New Mexico and California, Mexico severed diplomatic relations with the United States and refused to recognize the independence of Texas or the disputed Rio Grande border.[77] After the Mexican army ambushed General Taylor's forces across the Rio Grande border, Polk requested a declaration of war. His justification stated that Mexico "has passed the boundary for the United States, has invaded our territory, and shed American blood on American soil."[78] Despite the controversy, "Congress almost unanimously endorsed Polk's request for a declaration of war" to initiate the Mexican-American War in 1846.[79] Though there were many battles associated with the war, America launched a punitive expedition to invade Mexico through Veracruz in March 1847. The strategy was to "force Mexico to the negotiating table" by defeating Santa Anna's army and conquering the Mexican capitol in order to resolve the border dispute, secure the southern border, and negotiate the sale of New Mexico and California.[80] In a brilliant and aggressive punitive expedition lauded by none other than the Duke of Wellington, General Winfield Scott conquered Santa Anna's army in a punitive military campaign and occupied Mexico City in September of 1847.[81]

After Santa Anna and his army was defeated, an interim government was established in Mexico City. However, Scott "feared that a prolonged occupation would escalate the guerilla war and turn victory into disaster" and was vehemently opposed to

---

[77] Walter A. McDougall, *Promised Land, Crusader State*, 93.

[78] Allen R. Millett and Peter Maslowski, *For the Common Defense: A Military History of the United States* (New York: The Free Press, 1984), 138.

[79] Walter A. McDougall, *Promised Land, Crusader State*, 93.

[80] Millett and Maslowski, 146.

[81] Ibid., 149. According to Millet and Maslowski, the Duke of Wellington declared Scott "the greatest living soldier" and encouraged "English officers to study the Veracruz-to-Mexico City campaign, which he considered 'unsurpassed in military annals.'"

the annexation of Mexico.[82] Once an interim Mexican government was established in

occupied Mexico City, President Polk convinced the Mexicans to lay down their arms in

return for their sovereign independence and moved quickly to negotiate the legitimate

purchase of Mexico's North American lands, before a more radical "All Mexico

Movement" gathered sufficient political backing to support the full annexation of

Mexico.[83] Ultimately, Mexico ceded New Mexico and California to the United States for

$18.25 million in the 1848 Treaty of Guadalupe Hidalgo, which successfully ended the

occupation and the Mexican-American War.[84]

Ultimately, the strategy pursued in the Mexican-American War was *valid* because

it was *suitable, acceptable,* and *feasible*. The strategy was *suitable* because it secured

America's strategic ends, which included the resolution of the border dispute, security of

the southern border and the annexation of Mexican territory in North America,

particularly Texas and California, without long-term consequences to America's vital

national interests. Peace was reestablished and the border dispute was resolved between

the two nations in the 1848 Treaty of Guadalupe Hidalgo, which restored the security of

America's southern border and provided for the sale of Mexican territory. The United

States now possessed the territory to expand the nation into a coast-to-coast continental

territory with defendable natural ports on the west coast to expand trade in the Pacific

region.

---

[82] McDougall, *Throes of Democracy* (New York: Harper Collins Publishers Inc., 2008), 300.

[83] Ibid.

[84] Millett and Maslowski, 149. "Under the treaty's provisions the United States would pay Mexico $15 million and assume damage claims of its own citizens against Mexico totaling $3.25 million. In return Mexico would recognize the Rio Grande boundary and cede New Mexico and California."

The strategy utilized in the Mexican-American War was also *acceptable* as a punitive war against a militant neighboring nation bent on conquest. The defense of the southern border against Mexico's large mobilized army would have been difficult to achieve. Ultimately, the deteriorating international relations and security situation would have never been resolved without a military invasion. The war was justified as a war initiated by Mexican cross-border aggression, and the means of war were acceptable.

The strategy was also *feasible* because it was conducted as a punitive expedition with limited foreign policy objectives versus an idealistic crusade to defeat the military forces, conquer the national government, pacify the people, and annex the entire nation. The war was relatively quick, but it still cost the lives of 12,876 Americans (1,721 KIAs) and $58 million—approximately $1.4 billion in today's dollars.[85] However, the "All Mexico Movement" to annex Mexico would have led to a much costlier and bloodier protracted war to pacify the hostile Mexican population in order to attempt to export American liberty by force.

The Mexican-American War highlighted contrasting visions of American Expansionism and Manifest Destiny. A radical version of "Manifest Destiny" existed that turned away from the true tradition of Liberty. These radicals supported a progressive crusade of "liberating densely populated foreign countries" as a "regeneration of other cultures" in order to usher in the "blessings of American civilization."[86]

The "All Mexico Movement" sprang from these roots, which rejected the traditional notion that America "stand by Latin peoples fighting for liberty," and

---

[85] Millett and Maslowski, 150. "American deaths were 12,876 (5,909 regulars, 6,967 volunteers). As usual, disease and accidents, not bullets and bayonets, were the big killers. Only 1,721 men were killed in action or died of wounds."

[86] McDougall, *Promised Land, Crusader State*, 84.

proposed instead to "fight *against* those same people for the purpose of *teaching them liberty.*"[87] Invoking the righteous language of a religious crusade, radical "Manifest Destinarians" believed that "a free nation, which shows equal toleration and protection to all religions, and conquers only to bestow freedom, has no danger to fear."[88] However, it is far different to conquer an external aggressor to liberate a nation than it is to conquer the people to liberate them from themselves. This strategy calls for unacceptable means because the decision to conquer, kill, force or coerce the people violates the mandate for "equal protection" and is incompatible to the very nature of liberty.

However, Commodore Robert F. Stockton passionately called for the deployment of 50,000 troops in Mexico—five times the original invasion force at Veracruz—to establish an independent republic in Mexico.[89]

> If I were now the sovereign authority…I would prosecute this war for the express purpose of redeeming Mexico from misrule and civil strife….we have a duty before God which we cannot—we must not—evade. The priceless boon of civil and religious liberty has been confided to us as trustees. I would insist, if the war were to be prolonged for fifty years, and cost money enough to demand from each of us each year the half of all that we possess, I would still insist that the inestimable blessings of civil and religious liberty should be guaranteed to Mexico. We must not shrink from this solemn duty….I would insist, cost what it may, on the establishment of a permanent, independent republic in Mexico….I would, with a magnanimous and kindly hand, gather these wretched people within the fold of republicanism.[90]

---

[87] Ibid., 95-6.

[88] Ibid., 84. This is an idealistic illusion in order to provide a form of moral justification. In a war to "conquer only to bestow freedom," the greatest challenge is to know who you are trying to conquer and who you are trying to free, but as soon as the decision is made "equal protection" has been violated. As the old saying goes, "One man's freedom fighter is another man's terrorist."

[89] Samuel John Bayard, *A Sketch of the Life of Com. Robert F. Stockton* (New York: Derby and Jackson, 1856), 177, The Library of Congress Internet Archive, http://www.archive.org/details/sketchoflifeofco00baya (Accessed March 1, 2012).

[90] Ibid., 177-78. Commodore Stockton was the Commander of the squadron in the Pacific, and the Commander in chief of land forces in California during the Mexican-American War, who became a New Jersey Senator.

Though the Polk administration rejected calls for action of this kind, the belief that America must intervene to impose a "state of progressive civilization" or else Mexico would "relapse into degraded barbarism" continued to run as an undercurrent in the nation.[91] Evidence of this is the fact that these beliefs were very similar to the justification of "benevolent assimilation" later used in the Philippine-American War in the period of Progressive Imperialism.

However, there is a fundamental flaw in the logic because *civil order* imposed by force rather than established as a natural result of liberty and consent is not conducive to *civil liberty*. Civil liberty cannot be established without the free consent of the people, and the true consent of the people cannot coexist with coercion or force. Therefore, this strategy supporting the All Mexico Movement would not have been *valid* because it would not have been *acceptable* in accordance with the American principle of *popular sovereignty* and *civil liberty*. However, much of the same ideological beliefs of the All Mexico Movement would later surface again in the Progressive Movement.

Ultimately, the more realistic and limited objectives of the Mexican-American War resulted in success because American Expansionism finally secured a coast-to-coast, continental United States. However, these new territories also fractured both American Liberty and the Union—the two most vital of the vital national interests—in the process. The divisive debate whether this new territory would promote slavery or freedom tore the United States apart in the Civil War. "Manifest Destiny made disunity manifest."[92]

---

[91] Ibid., 179.

[92] Millett and Maslowski, 150.

The Civil War: Two Competing Visions of Grand Strategy and Foreign Policy

The Civil War was a very complex war that demonstrated the powerful and fundamentally different beliefs that fueled the horrific conflict. Certainly, different perspectives on state sovereignty and slavery were strong contributing factors. Though the specific reasons for the war are debatable, few historians "deny that the immediate question of whether the newly acquired land would be slave or free played a significant role in shattering the nation."[93] McDougall describes the Civil War as a manifestation of a fundamental split in the "American Civil Religion."[94] He defines the core issue as an "insoluble dispute over the meaning of Liberty at home."[95] Therefore, the Civil War illustrates the fundamentally different grand strategies and foreign policies for securing American Liberty pursued by the Union and the Confederacy.

President Lincoln fought to preserve the heritage of the Founding Fathers—the Constitution, the nation's Union, and their hard won Liberty at home—through a "birth of new freedom." The Union staunchly maintained the foreign policy tradition of Unilateralism by unequivocally opposing European intervention in the Civil War. The Union also protected the American System by opposing the French imperial [Louis Napoleon] campaign to conquer and control Mexico. Additionally, Expansionism was further fueled through the "transcontinental railroad, land-grant colleges, and the Homestead Act."[96]

In contrast, the Confederacy rejected the Founding Fathers concept of civil liberty and equality by rebelling against the Union and supplanting the Constitution that had

---

[93] Ibid.

[94] McDougall, *The Constitutional History of U.S. Foreign Policy*, 14.

[95] McDougall, *Promised Land, Crusader State,* 97.

[96] Ibid.

established and secured American Liberty. The Confederacy was self-described as "one of the greatest revolutions in the annals of the world," which supposedly "preserved the essentials of the old constitution," but embraced and justified the continuation of slavery.[97] The Confederacy was not based on the fundamental principles of liberty and the belief that "all men are created equal," which was espoused by the Founding Fathers in the Declaration of Independence.[98] The Confederacy also violated both Unilateralism and the American System by seeking British and French support against the Union, which would have also jeopardized Expansionism due to the reintroduction of European imperial interference and competition on the continent. However, the Confederacy viewed these breaks from American tradition as a new vision for America with "no obstacle in the way" of continued "upward and onward *progress*."[99]

Ultimately, the Union's victory over the Confederacy preserved America's way of life and founding documents, but these kind of *progressive* undercurrents of the nation continued to grow stronger. Unfortunately, the popularly supported Progressive

---

[97] Henry Cleveland, *Alexander H. Stephens, in Public and Private: With Letters and Speeches, Before, During, and Since the War,* (Philadelphia: National Publishing Company, 1866), 718, Hathi Trust Digital Library, http://babel.hathitrust.org/cgi/pt?view=image;size=75;id=uc1.b60934;page=root;seq=1 (Accessed 20 January 2012).

[98] Ibid., 721. Alexander Stephens, Vice President of the Confederacy stated in a speech in Savannah on 21 March 1861: "The new [Confederate] constitution has put at rest, *forever*, all the agitating questions relating to our peculiar institution—African slavery as it exists amongst us—the proper status of the negro in our form of civilization. This was the immediate cause of the late rupture and present revolution....The prevailing ideas entertained by him [Thomas Jefferson] and most of the leading statesmen at the time of the formation of the old constitution, were that the enslavement of the African was in violation of the laws of nature; that it was *wrong in principle*, socially, morally, and politically. It [slavery] was an evil they [the Founding Fathers] knew not well how to deal with, but the general opinion of the men of that day was that, somehow or other in the order of Providence, the institution would be evanescent and pass away. This idea, though not incorporated in the constitution, was the prevailing idea at that time. Those ideas, however, were fundamentally wrong. They rested upon the assumption of the equality of races. This was an error....Our new government is founded upon exactly the opposite idea; its foundations are laid, its corner-stone rests, upon the great truth that the negro is not equal to the white man; that slavery—subordination to the superior race—is his natural and normal condition....This truth has been slow in the process of its development, like all other truths in the various departments of science."

[99] Ibid., 726.

Movement, which had competed with foreign policy traditions in the 19th century, began to dominate policy in the 20th century. As the United States responded to increasing threats across the globe, her rise in power presented a challenge in and of itself. In many ways, power had the same effect on the United States that it has over all men; it corrupted American Liberty. Ultimately, the Progressive Movement shifted American grand strategy away from the foreign policy traditions of the Founding Fathers.

America's Modern Foreign Policy Traditions

America's more modern foreign policy traditions—Progressive Imperialism, Wilsonianism/Liberal Internationalism, Containment, and Global Meliorism— were established after 1898, during a period of tremendous change in the strategic environment. However, with the exception of Containment, these traditions departed from the original foreign policy traditions that defined American grand strategy during the first century of the United States. These traditions rejected America's traditional identity and role in the world, as well as some of the fundamental assumptions of human nature that were foundational to the design of the Constitution. The radical break from the original foreign policy traditions was primarily based on the theoretical ideology of the Progressive Movement.

The Progressive Movement: A Radical Break from American Tradition

The Progressive Movement had steadily built popular support in the United States to diverge away from the American foreign policy traditions in 1898. The ideology and assumptions directly conflicted with the tradition of American Liberty, which meant,

"Liberty at home, not crusades to change the world."[100] However, the Progressive Movement represented a powerful alignment of religious and secular ideologies that fueled the American popular support and national impetus for a foreign policy shift towards Progressive Imperialism, which served as an ideological foundation for Wilsonianism/Liberal Internationalism and Global Meliorism.

The Progressive Movement was fueled by "progressive mainstream Protestants" who embraced a Social Gospel that emphasized "works over faith...and heaven on earth as well as above."[101] The Social Gospel movement believed that the "purpose of America was to realize the Kingdom of God" and that "Progressive reforms (to be capped by Prohibition) were purifying Americans to make them worthy of their calling."[102] This growing Protestant sect became more politically influential in the period of Progressive Imperialism as their "church attendance soared 75 percent in the decade after 1895."[103] Ironically, this religious ideology was surprisingly congruent with the secular views of Social Darwinism, which based social progress on the continuing evolution of humanity through racial competition in the fight for survival and dominance.

Reverend Josiah Strong passionately articulated this convergence of American nationalistic religious and secular beliefs during this period in his best-selling book, *Our*

---

[100] McDougall, *Promised Land, Crusader State*, 118.

[101] Ibid., 104, 121. The ideological foundations of the Social Gospel were shaped by the "influence of Darwinian evolution and the 'higher criticism' of the Bible," which discounted the doctrine of original sin and opened the door for human perfectibity. However, the Bible does not support these progressive beliefs or the utopian view of a heaven on earth common in the "secular millenarianism of the Social Gospel." The "Christian Scriptures describe all earthly kingdoms as the devil's domain and history as a spiral toward the apocalypse."

[102] Ibid., 123, 128.

[103] Ibid., 104

Country, first published in 1885.[104] He described Americans as a "race of unequaled energy, with all of the majesty of numbers and the might of wealth behind it—the representative, let us hope, of the largest liberty, the purest Christianity, the highest civilization—having developed peculiarly aggressive traits calculated to impress its institutions upon mankind, will spread itself across the earth."[105] Strong continues with an unmistakable Darwinian element to his ideology: "And can anyone doubt that the result of this competition of races will be the 'survival of the fittest'?....Nothing can save the inferior race but a ready and pliant assimilation."[106] Therefore, the Social Gospel was combined with secular Social Darwinism and racial Anglo-Saxonism to form a powerful nation-wide ideological belief that Americans were "destined to dispossess many weaker races, assimilate others, and mold the remainder, until, in a very true and important sense, it has Anglo-Saxonized mankind."[107]

Progressivism continued to become more secular into the next century as it morphed into a social science. Hebert Croly, founder of the progressive periodical, *The New Republic*, was recognized as the "chief ideologist" of progressivism during the period.[108] Croly contrasts *progressive* democracy with his perspective of the traditional "live-and-let-live" mindset of America's democratic republic in his 1915 book, *Progressive Democracy*.

---

[104] Ibid., 105.

[105] Josiah Strong, *Our Country: Its Possible Future and Its Present Crisis* (New York: The Baker & Taylor Co., 1885), 175, Internet Archive: American Libraries, http://www.archive.org/details/ourcountryitspo07strogoog (accessed March 1, 2012).

[106] Ibid.

[107] McDougall, *Promised Land, Crusader State*, 178.

[108] Ibid., 120.

If the prevailing legalism and a repressive moral code are associated with the rule of live-and-let-live, the *progressive* democratic faith finds its consummation rather in the rule of *live-and-help-live*....The underlying assumption of live-and-help-live is an ultimate collectivism,...which makes individual fulfillment depend upon the fulfillment of other lives and upon that of society as a whole. The *obligation* of mutual assistance is fundamental. The opportunities of mutual assistance are inexhaustible. Wherever the lives of other people are frustrated, we are responsible for the frustration just in so far as we have failed to do what we could for their liberation; and we can always do something on behalf of liberty....We cannot liberate ourselves without seeking to liberate them...Thus the progressive democratic faith...is at bottom a spiritual expression of the mystical unity of human nature.[109]

This moral obligation and mutual responsibility to assist and liberate others is a central theme in progressivism. Croly explained: "Democracy has assumed an express responsibility for the achievement of the stupendous task of making this world into a place in which *more human beings will lead better lives* than they have hitherto had an opportunity of doing," which requires the "*subordination*, to a very considerable extent, of *individual interests* and desires to the requirements of *social welfare*."[110] This fueled the popular movements for social reform at home and abroad in order to *progress* the human race towards perfection.

There are several problems with this progressive view of democracy. First, human nature is governed by self-interest and a theory based on the subordination of self-interest is idealistic at best. Secondly, this ideology is based on the premise that the United States "can, should and must reach out to help other nations share in the American dream"—American Liberty. This premise is based on three core assumptions: 1) the "American model is universally valid," 2) the United States is morally obligated to help

---

[109] Herbert D. Croly, *Progressive Democracy* (New York: The Macmillan Company, 1915), 426-27, American Libraries Internet Archive, http://www.archive.org/details/progressivedemo04crolgoog (Accessed 20 January 2012).

[110] Ibid., 406.

other nations embrace it; and 3) American Liberty *at home* depends on freeing other nations from poverty and tyranny *abroad*.[111] These assumptions are certainly questionable, but the flawed assumption of human nature is the most fundamental.

This idealistic assumption of the perfectibility of human nature—a critical component of utopianism—directly conflicted with the traditional realistic worldview of a depraved and unchanging human nature held by the Founding Fathers. Even Croly seems to question the feasibility of this idealistic assumption in his 1911 book, *The Promise of American Life*: "For better or worse, democracy cannot be disentangled from the aspiration toward *human perfectibility*, and hence from the adoption of measures looking in the direction of realizing such an aspiration. It may be that the attempt will not seriously be made, or that, if it is, *nothing will come of it*."[112] Therefore, *progressive democracy* calls for action based on an idealistic assumption of human perfectibility.

The idealism embedded in the core of progressivism is further demonstrated by the foundation of *faith* required for social progress in a democracy.

> The faith which must sustain a democracy is *faith in human values*, individual and social, not in the accomplishment of specific *results*. The assumption of a large and a genuine *risk* is inseparable from a loyal participation in the enterprise; and any success which may be secured will have to be purchased by *sacrifices* as considerable and as genuine as the risks. Faith is necessary and constructive, precisely because the situation *demands both risks and sacrifices*, and because the readiness to incur the risk and make the sacrifices is an essential part of political character in a democracy."[113]

---

[111] McDougall, *Promised Land, Crusader State*, 173.

[112] Hebert Croly, *The Promise of American Life* (New York: The MacMillan Company, 1911), 454, Google Books, http://books.google.com/books/about/The_Promise_of_American_Life.html?id=3BASAAAAYAAJ (Accessed January 20, 2012).

[113] Croly, *Progressive Democracy*, 170.

Therefore, the strategy of progressive democracy focused on faith, which drove idealistic *ends* based on human values versus specific results or national interests. This strategy also demands *risk* and sacrifice as necessary *means* with faith as the primary mitigation. Thus, this progressive mindset cannot be effectively translated into strategy, because it is antithetical to strategic theory.

The Founding Fathers initially committed the same strategic error of basing their political strategy on a false assumption, but they corrected their strategic mistake. They relied on faith in human nature in their strategic design of the Articles of Confederation. However, they learned a valuable lesson from their failure to achieve the expected *results*—faith in human values or ideals does not trump the reality of human nature. Based on the wisdom and judgment gained from this practical lesson, the Founding Fathers did not base the strategic design of the Constitution on faith in human nature. Instead, they based it solidly on a strategy to institutionally mitigate the reality of human nature in order to achieve the desired strategic *results*—civil liberty and order. Therefore, it was a *mistake* to found strategy on a false assumption based on the expected hope of what human nature or the world should be, which resulted in strategic consequences unmitigated by the strategy. However, it is foolish to reject the lessons of history and practical experience and expect different strategic results. Nonetheless, progressive leaders rejected the reality of practical experience or the hard lessons of the past and replaced it with a theoretical ideology unsoundly founded on an idealistic and theoretical faith in human progress.

The potent convergence of faith-based and theoretical progressive beliefs represented a powerful political alliance between religious and secular factions in the

American *extended republic*, which served as the ideological core for a dominant coalition majority that fueled the popular support for the nation to break away from America's traditional foreign policies in 1898. This popular progressive movement supported the reform work necessary for Progressive Imperialism. This ideology also shaped and informed the later progressive foreign policy traditions of Wilsonianism/ Liberal Internationalism and Global Meliorism. The next sections will analyze and criticize the effectiveness of these progressive strategies and the strategic risk that was exposed in execution of these foreign policy traditions.

Progressive Imperialism

Progressive Imperialism represented a shift in the United States from a respectable unilateral defensive posture that promoted American Liberty and secured vital national interests to an aggressive foreign policy to transplant American Liberty into new colonies outside the continental U.S. America's Progressive Imperialism resulted from a powerful combination of the Progressive Movement and the strategic response to the more threatening strategic environment in the late 1800s and early 1900s—American colonial expansion. America was a world power by 1900 in every way except militarily. Consequently, the nation was far more vulnerable than it is today. Of the European nations, America's large population of 71 million people was second only to Russia.[114] America was an "economic superpower" in the late 1800's. "Its industrial production became the greatest in the world by surpassing Great Britain around 1885."[115] However, America maintained a small standing army of less than 27,000 that was legislatively

---

[114] McDougall, *Promised Land, Crusader State,* 102.

[115] Ibid.

constrained by Congress, which was tiny compared to the powerful European countries: Great Britain—236,000; France—544,000; Germany—545,000; and Russia—896,000.[116] Additionally, the "optimistic, liberal spirit that characterized Europe in the 1850s and '60s gave way to a brooding mood of impending conflict informed by Social Darwinist notions of racial competition and survival of the fittest."[117]

A resurgence of European imperialism in the late 1870s ushered in a more threatening "world of fierce commercial and naval competitors," which demanded a strategic response to secure vital national interests.[118] American international trade via the high seas was vulnerable and largely dependent on the protection of Great Britain, which demanded a shift in strategy to protect the vital national interests of the United States. The threat galvanized the national will to build a modern, steel "two-ocean fleet" for the U.S. Navy.[119] However, the navy was still comparatively small with only five battleships in 1896, though seven additional ships were in construction. In comparison, "Great Britain had 45 (with 12 under construction), France 29 and Germany 21."[120] These facts do not indicate a nation on the verge of an imperialistic campaign of conquest. However, America required a U.S. Navy capable of securing international sea-lanes threatened by the growing imperial fleets in order to support America's vital commercial trade throughout the world. According to Captain A. T. Mahan's seminal book, *Influence of Sea Power on History*, colonies "facilitate and enlarge the operations

---

[116] Christopher J. Fettweis, "Dangerous Revisionism: On the Founders, 'Neocons' and the Importance of History," *Orbis: A Journal of World Affairs.* Volume 53, no. 3 (Summer 2009): 518-19.

[117] McDougall, *Promised Land, Crusader State,* 104.

[118] Ibid.

[119] Ibid.

[120] Fettweis, 520.

of shipping" and "protect it by multiplying points of safety" and naval power in the "seas often beset with enemies" and "lawlessness."[121] Therefore, colonies in the Caribbean and Pacific had to be secured to serve as naval bases and coaling stations to effectively support the "two-ocean fleet" required by the U.S. Navy to secure America's vital national interests.[122] In essence, America's imperial initiatives were strategic *ends* designed to secure vital national interests in response to the elevated threats in the strategic environment. However, the Progressive Movement shaped and fueled the aggressive and militant *ways* and *means* utilized for colonial expansion, which resembled an ideological crusade.

Despite the apparent "aberration" in American history, certain aspects of the imperial initiatives from 1898-1917 were consistent with the earlier foreign policy traditions of Unilateralism, the American System and Expansionism.[123] The United States maintained Unilateralism by continuing to avoid all entangling alliances with the imperial powers. The United States also "consistently preempted European involvements" in the Caribbean and Pacific region in the tradition of the American System.[124] In fact, Theodore Roosevelt reinforced the American System with the Roosevelt Corollary to the Monroe Doctrine, which asserted that the U.S. would use military force to "exercise international police power" in order to protect American vital

---

[121] Captain A. T. Mahan, *The Influence of Sea Power upon History, 1660-1783*, (New York: Dover Publications, Inc., 1987), 28.

[122] McDougall, *Promised Land, Crusader State,* 104.

[123] Ibid., 118.

[124] Ibid., 114, 117. For example, a potentially entangling agreement with Britain granting an "equal say in any isthmian canal project" was renegotiated in the 1901 Hay-Pauncefote Treaty, which "granted the United States exclusive rights to dig and defend the Panama canal."

national interests in the Western Hemisphere.[125] However, the Western Hemisphere was expanded towards the Pacific territories even though "the water boundary where America stopped and Asia began was never defined."[126] The strategic goal of Expansionism was to secure a relatively contiguous security zone consisting of a geographical array of "bases and ports, which, if possessed by foreign imperial powers, might pose a threat to the Panama Canal or sea lanes plied by American ships."[127] Therefore, American bases and ports were secured in various ways in Cuba, Puerto Rico, Panama, Hawaii, Alaska, Samoa, Guam, and the Philippines. However, the strategy to secure these bases and ports—Progressive Imperialism—was a radical strategic change in American foreign policy.

Progressive Imperialism transformed the tradition of American Liberty, which defined American identity and *domestic policy* at home, into a progressive ideological crusade that defined America's identity and *foreign policy* abroad. However, the *means* employed were not *acceptable* or consistent with America's traditional grand strategy. In other words, the *ends* did not justify the *means*. Despite these issues, the Progressive Movement provided the popular support for this crusade to be broadly accepted and passionately pursued by Americans. The foreign policy transformation to Progressivism manifested itself most clearly in three distinct historical events that happened in 1898. The first was Cuban War of Independence, which was the first time in American history

---

[125] Theodore Roosevelt, "Transcript of Theodore Roosevelt's Corollary to the Monroe Doctrine (1905)," Our Documents: 100 Milestone Documents from the National Archives, http://ourdocuments.gov/doc.php?flash=true&doc=56&page=transcript (accessed September, 12, 2011).

[126] McDougall, *Promised Land, Crusader State,* 117.

[127] Ibid., 117-18.

that the nation went to war to support a foreign revolution.[128] The second was the annexation of the Republic of Hawaii despite the majority opposition of the native people. The third was the Philippine-American War, which was a counter-insurgency war with the progressive "mission to transplant American civilization" into a foreign nation.[129]

The intervention in Cuba during the Spanish-American War changed a long-standing policy of strict neutrality in revolutions, in accordance with the American Liberty tradition. In 1898, the United States decided to use force in a crusade to support Cuba's revolution after Spain repeatedly rebuffed diplomatic pressure to negotiate an armistice. At President McKinley's request, Congress passed a joint resolution that "declared Cuba independent, insisted that Spanish forces withdraw, [and] authorized the president to use force to ensure these results."[130] In fact, Senate support was contingent on justifying the war in the name of liberty. Senator John C. Spooner articulated the sentiment best: "We intervene, not for conquest, not for aggrandizement, not because of the Monroe doctrine; we intervene for humanity's sake; we intervene to gain security for the future; we intervene to aid a people who have suffered every form of tyranny and who have made a desperate struggle to be free."[131] However, the joint resolution along with

---

[128] Ibid., 118.

[129] Ibid., 120.

[130] Ibid., 110-11. The McKinley administration was under tremendous public and political pressure to intervene in Cuba, which became feverish after the mysterious explosion of the USS Maine in the Havana Harbor.

[131] Arthur J. Dodge, "Outburst of Patriotic Sentiment," The National Magazine, Vol. VIII, (April – September, 1898), 274, http://books.google.com/books?id=MYzNAAAAMAAJ& (accessed May 25, 2012).

the Teller Amendment rejected any notion of annexing Cuba.[132] Americans eagerly

fought the Spanish-American War to end Spanish colonial oppression in support of *Cuba*

libre! Spain was quickly defeated and signed a treaty that ceded control of Puerto Rico,

Guam and the Philippines to the United States. Cuba was granted independence, but only

with significant caveats that limited Cuba's sovereignty over foreign policy and trade via

the Platt Amendment and the Cuban-American Treaty, which also established a U.S.

naval base at Guantanamo Bay.[133] Cuba won its independence with American assistance,

but ended up as a "virtual protectorate" of the United States.[134]

Coercion was also used to secure the annexation of the Republic of Hawaii in

1898. In 1893, President Cleveland refused to support the annexation of the independent

Republic of Hawaii, because he would not support the overthrow of a sovereign

government or annexing a people against their consent.[135] However, after growing

---

[132] Teller, Henry M., "Teller Amendment, 19 April 1898," Library of Congress, The World of 1898: The Spanish-American War, http://www.loc.gov/rr/hispanic/1898/teller html (accessed May 25, 2012). The United States "hereby disclaims any disposition of intention to exercise sovereignty, jurisdiction, or control over said island except for pacification thereof, and asserts its determination, when that is accomplished, to leave the government and control of the island to its people."

[133] Platt, Orville., "Platt Amendment, February 1901," Library of Congress, The World of 1898: The Spanish-American War, http://www.loc.gov/rr/hispanic/1898/teller html (accessed May 25, 2012). It gave the United States "the right to intervene for the preservation of Cuban independence, the maintenance of a government adequate for the protection of life, property, and individual liberty..."

[134] McDougall, *Promised Land, Crusader State*, 114-15.

[135] U.S. Code, Title 42, Chapter 122, "Native Hawaiian Health Care," Section 11701. Findings, 01/03/2012 (112-90), The Office of the Law Revision Counsel, http://uscode house.gov/download/pls/42C122.txt (accessed 25 May, 2012). "The Congress finds that:...In the year 1893.... the United States Minister and the naval representative of the United States caused armed naval forces of the United States to invade the sovereignHawaiian Nation in support of the overthrow of the indigenous and lawful Government of Hawaii....In a message to Congress on December 18, 1893, then President Grover Cleveland reported fully and accurately on these illegal actions, and acknowledged that by these acts, described by the President as acts of war, [and] the government of a peaceful and friendly people was overthrown." In 1898, the United States annexed Hawaii through the Newlands Resolution without the consent of or compensation to the indigenous people of Hawaii or their sovereign government who were thereby denied the mechanism for expression of their inherent sovereignty through self-government and self-determination, their lands and ocean resources."

Japanese immigration and continued pressure from Japan, the House Foreign Affairs Committee recommended that: "Annexation, and that alone will securely maintain American control in Hawaii."[136] The Senate blocked the annexation treaty because of a petition representing a majority of native Hawaiian's against it. Undeterred, President McKinley asked Congress for a joint resolution rather than the more legitimate treaty to annex the Republic of Hawaii because it did not require the ratification of the Senate. The independent Republic of Hawaii was annexed in 1898 against the consent of the majority of native Hawaiians.[137] The coercive *means* employed in the annexation of Hawaii were contrary to the central premise of the freedom of natural liberty and consent, which is central to popular sovereignty. However, Hawaii was at least granted the status of an incorporated territory, which meant the citizens were protected by the Constitution. However, the Philippines, Puerto Rico and Guam were annexed as unincorporated dependencies, which denied them not only the right to self-determination, but also the equal protection of the Constitution.

Despite the idealistic rhetoric, Progressive Imperialism was inconsistent with the Constitution and the tradition of American Liberty. The Constitution outlines provisions for the admission of new states including a guarantee of a "Republican Form of

---

[136] Henry Watterson, *History of the Spanish-American War; Embracing A Complete Review of Our Relations with Spain* (San Francisco: E. D. Bronson & Co., 1898), 286, Internet Archive, University of California, California Digital Library, http://archive.org/stream/spanishamwar00wattrich (accessed May 25, 2012). A large section of the committee report is extracted, which explain the reasoning. The resultant Joint Resolution is also provided in full in the text.

[137] U.S. Code, Title 42, Chapter 122, Section 11701. "In 1898, the United States annexed Hawaii through the Newlands Resolution without the consent of or compensation to the indigenous people of Hawaii or their sovereign government who were thereby denied the mechanism for expression of their inherent sovereignty through self-government and self-determination, their lands and ocean resources."

Government.[138] The U.S. did not incorporate these new territories or accept them as

States. Therefore, the government had no Constitutional authority to guarantee, much

less forcefully impose, a republican form of government on the new territories. *The*

Federalist Papers confirms that this provision of Constitutional "authority extends no

further than to a *guarantee* of a republican form of government, which supposes a pre-

existing government of the [same] form which is to be guaranteed….The only restriction

imposed on them is that they shall not exchange republican for anti-republican

constitutions."[139] There was no implication that the federal government would impose a

republican form of government on the territory. The obvious intent was that the federal

government would provide protection to ensure that the republican form of government

remained viable during a contingency, such as an insurrection. New territories could be

annexed or apply to be annexed as states based on their consent and the approval of

Congress.[140] However, despite the idealistic promises of American liberty, the consent of

the people had little to do with the process. Instead, the "imperialist compromise" was to

annex territory, control the ground, impose government, and even raise the flag, but

"deny that the Constitution followed the flag."[141]

---

[138] The U.S. Constitution, Article IV, Section 3 states: "New States may be admitted by the Congress into this Union" and "The Congress shall have Power to dispose of and make all needful Rules and Regulations respecting the Territory or other Property belonging to the United States." Section 4 states: "The United States shall guarantee to every State in this Union a Republican Form of Government, and shall protect each of them against Invasion; and on Application of the Legislature, or the Executive (when the Legislature cannot be convened) against domestic violence."

[139] Hamilton, Madison, and Jay, 271-72.

[140] The Republic of Texas' request for statehood and the long and controversial annexation of Texas as an official state of the United States is an example.

[141] McDougall, *Promised Land, Crusader State,* 119.

The Philippine-American War: A War of Progressive Imperialism

The Philippine-American War serves as the most graphic example of Progressive Imperialism and the unacceptable means employed to "transplant American civilization." The Philippines were annexed after the Spanish-American War. However, instead of recognizing their independence, the United States colonized the Philippines in a war against the Filipinos based on an idealistic "belief that American power, guided by a secular and religious spirit of service, could remake foreign societies."[142] The idealistic—not to mention arrogant—assumption of Progressive Imperialism is that America has the "power, wisdom, charity, patience, right, and duty to rule over foreigners until they were judged mature enough for self-rule."[143] President McKinley believed that America needed to "educate the Filipinos, and uplift and civilize and Christianize them." The Filipinos were denied self-determination and independence because it was believed that they were not ready and would fall victim to "anarchy or colonization by Japan or Germany."[144] Therefore, the United States paid Spain $20 million and annexed the Philippines with the unilateral declaration that America would pursue the "benevolent assimilation" of the Filipinos.[145]

The reality of war replaced the idealistic process of transplanting American civilization in a "benevolent assimilation" when the Filipinos chose to fight for their own liberty and independence rather than consent to the *coercive* assimilation. Tragically, America *chose* to fight against the very people they supposedly had freed from the

---

[142] Ibid., 120.

[143] McDougall, *The Constitutional History of U.S. Foreign Policy*, 19.

[144] McDougall, *Promised Land, Crusader State,* 112.

[145] Max Boot, *The Savage Wars of Peace: Small Wars and the rise of American Power* (New York: Basic Books, 2003), 106.

tyranny of the Spanish Empire. President McKinley had mandated that the "insurgents must recognize the authority of the United States" and the military commander was given authorization to "Use whatever means in your judgment are necessary to this end."[146] In order to carry out the American policy, the Army was forced to impose martial law and fight a brutal three and a half year counterinsurgency campaign before the Filipino guerillas were defeated. In actuality, the United States merely imposed a different kind of tyranny—the tyranny of the American "Empire." Eventually, American benevolence earned coerced popular support, once the surviving revolutionary leadership was imbedded into the American-led representative civil government, which was sufficient to sustain the peace.[147]

However, the cost in human life was extremely high for a war of choice that was supposedly justified as being in the best interests of the Filipino people. Ultimately, "4,200 American soldiers were killed in action and 2,800 were wounded." The toll on the Filipinos was exponentially higher, since approximately "20,000 Filipino soldiers died, while an alleged 200,000 civilians died from famine, disease and war-related calamities."[148] Despite being described as "benevolent assimilation, the war was more aptly described by one American general as an "unholy war" and another general officer admitted that the "U.S. had ruthlessly suppressed in the Philippines an insurrection better justified than was our Revolution of glorious memory."[149] These facts and eyewitness

---

[146] Millett and Maslowski, 289.

[147] Ibid., 296.

[148] Ibid.

[149] Ibid., 296-7.

perspectives beg a critical question. Did the ends justify the means in this *progressive* war?

It is difficult to justify the *means* employed to institute these progressive reforms as *acceptable*. The militant means chosen and stubborn pursuit of a war that caused the deaths of several hundred thousand Americans and Filipinos represented an unacceptably high price to pay to achieve a progressive goal to "transplant American civilization." It certainly did not represent "benevolent assimilation" in the tradition of American Liberty and popular sovereignty. The means chosen were also very expensive. The war cost the United States an additional $400 million for the three-year war—20 times what the United States paid Spain for the Philippines—which is equivalent to an estimated $10 billion in today's dollars.[150] This is also almost eight times more than the punitive Mexican-American War cost the United States, which also questions the long-term *feasibility* of protracted counter-insurgency wars to install or reform a government.[151] Despite the enormous long-term investment and cost in human lives, the Philippines did not gain their independence until 1946—almost 44 years after the war ended. Ultimately, Progressive Imperialism must be judged an *invalid* strategy because the means were *unacceptable* to the traditions of American Liberty and popular sovereignty.

The national movement to secure colonies through Progressive Imperialism ended in the early 1900s after U.S. national security needs were met, but America still maintained a *progressive* foreign policy despite the *unacceptable means* required. The

---

[150] Ibid., 296.

[151] McDougall, *Promised Land, Crusader State,* 114. Additionally, this high cost does not include the enormous follow-on cost of developing an undeveloped nation. After hostilities ceased, Americans dutifully began the program of progressive reforms to modernize and Americanize the Philippines. "At considerable public and private expense they built ports, roads, railroads, schools, and hospitals, instituted land reform and experimented with economic policies they would later try at home" in programs such as the New Deal.

progressive mission abroad continued in the colonies gained after the Spanish-American

War. Despite the conflicting evidence as to the effectiveness and contradictions of

progressive strategies, President Woodrow Wilson aggressively advanced the progressive

movement to the next level and ambitiously mobilized the nation to transform the entire

international community through his idealistic form of Liberal Internationalism.

Wilsonianism (Liberal Internationalism)

Wilsonianism was virtually defined in President Wilson's famous Fourteen Points

speech and the League of Nations Covenant, which were designed to be the "programme

of the world's peace" to make the "world secure once and for all" from war through the

cooperation and collective action of a league of nations .[152] Though often viewed as

idealistic, Akira Iriye defends Wilsonianism: "It was not so much idealism as

internationalism that informed Wilsonian thought, an internationalism solidly grounded

on shared interests of nations and on the aspirations of men and women everywhere

transcending national boundaries."[153] Based on America's own experience with the

sovereign states in the Articles of Confederation, the assumption of the shared interests of

sovereign states or nations has proven to be unstable ground to serve as a foundation for

unified, collective action—even under ideal conditions. Competing rather than shared

interests characterize human nature more accurately in the long-term. Wilsonianism is

idealistic because it does not realistically account for issues of self-interests and power

associated with human nature.

---

[152] Woodrow Wilson, "8 January, 1918: President Woodrow Wilson's Fourteen Points." Avalon Project: Documents in Law, History and Diplomacy, Lillian Goldman Law Library, Yale Law School. http://avalon.law.yale.edu/20th_century/wilson14.asp (accessed September 20, 2011).

[153] Akira Iriye, *The Cambridge History of American Foreign Relations*, vol. 3, *The Globalizing of America, 1913-1945* (Cambridge: Cambridge University Press, 1993), 72.

President Wilson's unrealistic idealism is evident in his 1916 "Peace Without Victory" speech, which was his attempt to end the war after his narrow reelection. He called for "the peoples of the countries now at war" to "renounce their ambitions" and "with one accord adopt the doctrine of President Monroe as the doctrine of the whole world." Europeans blasted Wilson for his naïve belief that words and fanciful wishes could deliver what they were fighting to achieve. The incoming French Premiere, Georges Clemenceau, sarcastically ridiculed the American president for his unrealistic optimism concerning human nature: "Never before has any political assembly heard so fine a sermon on what human beings might be capable of accomplishing if only they weren't *human*."[154] Therefore, the main source of Wilson's unrealistic idealism stems from a false assumption that discounts the depravity of human nature. Despite the most fervent belief to the contrary, words do not deter or sway powerful men bent on subterfuge or conquest; these men only understand and respect power. Thus, Wilson and Wilsonians are criticized for their "naïve belief that power politics could be trumped by world opinion or abolished by the stroke of a pen."[155]

President Wilson also unilaterally declared in his Fourteen Points speech, that the "general association of nations....cannot be separated in interest or divided in purpose. We stand together until the end."[156] However, even the Allies had divergent interests and would not accept the armistice until reservations to the Fourteen Points were conceded. President Wilson compromised repeatedly to win the other nation's acceptance of the

---

[154] Georges Clemenceau, Comments on Wilson's "Peace Without Victory" Speech quoted in J. W. Schulte Nordholt, *Woodrow Wilson: A Life for World Peace*, trans. by Hebert H. Rowen (Berkeley: University of California Press, 1991), 289.

[155] McDougall, *Promised Land, Crusader State,* 125.

[156] Woodrow Wilson, "8 January, 1918: President Woodrow Wilson's Fourteen Points."

League of Nations Covenant, but was unable to get it ratified in the United States because of the significant reservations of the Senate.[157]

The Senate had numerous "reservations and amendments" concerning the League of Nations Covenant, particularly Article 10, which authorized the use of force. The Senate was determined to prevent this "new order" from undermining "the sovereignty and the Constitution of the United States and the Monroe Doctrine."[158] They proposed fourteen reservations and amendments. The Senate argued that the League was: 1) *idealistic* because it attempted to "freeze the global status quo" without accounting for power imbalances or national interests among the nations; 2) *ineffective* without force and thus was a league to "make war and not peace;" 3) *imprudent*, since the use of force was dictated by a "vague universal obligation" rather than by vital national interests; and 4) *unconstitutional* because it usurped the Congressional power to declare war.[159] When Wilson refused to compromise, the Senate refused to ratify the treaty, which eventually undermined the effectiveness of the League.

Some may argue that Presidents Franklin Roosevelt and Harry Truman succeeded in achieving the goals of Liberal Internationalism as an American foreign policy tradition where Wilson had failed. Ultimately, the United Nations did not achieve strategic success either. Senator Vandenberg's caveats to the U.N. Charter best express the Senate's continued support for a strong national defense, and the cautious and conditional support for liberal internationalism.

> I still believe that we can never again—regardless of collaborations—
> allow our national defense to deteriorate to anything like a point of

---

[157] McDougall, *Promised Land, Crusader State,* 139-40.

[158] Ibid., 144-45.

[159] Ibid., 141-43.

impotence....I want maximum American cooperation, consistent with *legitimate American interest*, with *constitutional process* and with collateral events that warrant it, to make the basic idea of Dumbarton Oaks [the United Nations] succeed....But, Mr. President, this also *requires whole-hearted reciprocity*. In honest candor, I think we should tell other nations that this glorious thing we contemplate is not and cannot be one-sided. I think we must say again that *unshared idealism is a menace* which we could not undertake to underwrite in the postwar world.[160]

The United Nations Charter was signed by the President and ratified by the Senate in 1945. However, the "whole-hearted reciprocity" never materialized and the hopes of greater peace were exposed as an "unshared idealism."

The United Nations, like the League of Nations, relied on an idealistic assumption of human nature, which led to an invalid strategy that was ineffective because of the divergent national interests and power politics of the member nations. The strategy of Wilsonianism/Liberal Internationalism *assumed* that the nations would reciprocate as if they were united in a community of consent—based on common interests, values and beliefs—and equally committed to the common good of the world community. The strategy *assumed* international unity, and, therefore, granted no real power to align national interests, check national actions, or balance national power.

Ultimately, the League of Nations and the United Nations failed for the same strategic reasons that the Articles of Confederation were ineffective. Even with the ideal conditions of the homogenous and united American community, the Articles of Confederation were ineffective because the federal government was not granted enough

---

[160] Arthur H. Vandenberg, "American Foreign Policy, January 10, 1945," *Congressional Record*, 79th Congress, 1st Session, *Congressional Record*, 79th Congress, 1st Session, 164-67, United States Senate, Senate.gov, http://www.senate.gov/artandhistory/history/resources/pdf/VandenbergSpeech.pdf (accessed 25 May, 2012).

power and sovereignty to directly govern the people and check state interests to promote and secure the national interests. In stark contrast, a true international community—based on common interests, values, and rights—simply did not exist in the world. To make matters worse, the League of Nations and the United Nations were granted virtually no power to govern international relations. Since no *true* power was granted to check sovereign nations, the nations were required to check each other through either war or the threat of war, which was counter to the strategic end of world peace. In the final analysis, Wilsonianism/Liberal Internationalism and the international organizations established to usher in world peace represented a strategic design even less effective than the Articles of Confederation. The strategy was plagued with *risk* because the *ends* were unrealistic due to *false assumptions*. The strategy was *invalid* because the ways and means—League of Nations and the United Nations—did not meet the *suitability* or *feasibility* tests, and any unilateral sacrifice of national sovereignty required would not have passed the *acceptability* test, particularly in the Senate.

The strategic *risk* introduced by this false assumption was eventually exposed. There was little advantage gained by these international organizations, since they were virtually powerless to resolve international conflict that could not be resolved by the nations themselves. International relations after World War I eventually degenerated into war—World War II. Likewise, the vision of a "new world order" under the United Nations collapsed under the reality of human nature and "power politics" in Europe and Asia, which ushered in the long struggle of the Cold War.[161] It is during this period of

---

[161] McDougall, *Promised Land, Crusader State,* 146.

worldwide ideological struggle that America turned to the more realistic foreign policy tradition of Containment.

Containment

After World War II, the United States was forced to use national power to *contain*—or more accurately, to balance against—the military and political aggression of the Soviet Union throughout world. The United Nations did not have the necessary international consent or consensus on the Security Council to be effective in securing and maintaining international order. Additionally, the United Nations was powerless to enforce international law or specific resolutions unless the member nations agreed to employ national power in the international police role. Therefore, the foreign policy tradition of Containment was developed to balance against Soviet aggression.

After World War II and the rise of the Soviet Union, Great Britain sought an alliance with the United States that Winston Churchill described as a "fraternal association of the English speaking peoples…a special relationship between the British Commonwealth and the United States."[162] Therefore, this strategic alliance represented a combination of national power to act as the world's international police power. The American-British alliance was envisioned to be the military foundation of the United Nations to protect the free world and the "only means by which this organization will achieve its full status and strength."[163] The United States was the only ally capable of stepping into Great Britain's role of maintaining the balance of power in Europe and

---

[162] Winston Churchill, "The Sinews of Peace," Speech at Westminister College, Fulton, Missouri, March 5, 1946, The Churchill Centre and Museum at the Churchill War Rooms, London, https://www.winstonchurchill.org/learn/speeches/speeches-of-winston-churchill/1946-1963-elder-statesman/120-the-sinews-of-peace (accessed 25 May, 2012).

[163] Ibid.

providing a stabilizing foundation for international order and free trade with her powerful navy.

In 1947, President Truman established the "Truman Doctrine," which called for a much larger world role for the United States to balance against Soviet aggression. Stalin consolidated Soviet power in Eastern Europe and established communist governments in Poland, Hungary, Romania, Bulgaria and Czechoslovakia. Stalin had also set his sights on Greece and Turkey, which would have destabilized the Middle East. Great Britain was incapable of providing aid so President Truman convinced Congress to provide $400 million along with military and civilian advisors to aid Greece and Turkey and prevent the development of another world war. This was a relative small investment to maintain the stability in the region, since the requested amount represented "only one tenth of one percent of the $341 billion spent in World War II."[164] However, the Truman Doctrine also became the foundation for America's role in the worldwide ideological clash between two competing ways of life. The Truman Doctrine defined the role of the United States and shaped the strategy of Containment in the Cold War.

> To ensure the peaceful development of nations, free from coercion, the United States has taken a leading part in establishing the United Nations.... I believe that it must be the policy of the United States to support free peoples who are resisting attempted subjugation by armed minorities or by outside pressures. I believe that we must assist free peoples to work out their own destinies in their own way. I believe that our help should be primarily through economic and financial aid which is essential to economic stability and orderly political processes....If we falter in our leadership, we may endanger the peace of the world – and we shall surely endanger the welfare of our own nation.[165]

---

[164] McDougall, *Promised Land, Crusader State,* 163.

[165] Harry S. Truman, "Truman Doctrine: President Harry S. Truman's Address Before a Joint Session of Congress, March 12, 1947," Avalon Project: Documents in Law, History and Diplomacy, Lillian Goldman Law Library, Yale Law School. http://avalon.law.yale.edu/20th_century/trudoc.asp (accessed September 20, 2011).

National interest and the strategic environment forced the United States to break with foreign policy tradition in order to form the 1949 North Atlantic Treaty Organization (NATO), "America's first permanent peacetime alliance."[166] On the surface, NATO would seem to represent an "entangling alliance," which President Washington warned against in his "Great Rule." However, the United States was now the dominant allied power, and the alliance actually enhanced national power and increased freedom of action to secure national interests. Ultimately, national interests and the more dangerous strategic environment required the alliance to restore the balance of power. The rise of the Soviet Union and relative weakness of Europe to check or balance the aggression and expansion of the communist empire forced the United States to intervene due to vital national interests. America required European and Asian "materials, markets and sea lanes" and could not allow Soviet or Communist domination of either Europe or Asia.[167] NATO, coupled with the Marshall Plan, served as the American means to "extend the Monroe Doctrine across the Atlantic to buttress Europe's balance of power" against the Soviet Union, particularly after the rapid decline of Great Britain's imperial power.[168] However, Containment represented a broader strategic response beyond the Truman Doctrine, NATO and the Marshall Plan.

The Truman Doctrine established America's initial role in the Cold War, but Containment was not yet a mature or *feasible* strategy. George Kennan provided much of the intellectual rationale and coined the term "containment" in his "Mr. X" Article.

---

[166] Ibid., 165.

[167] Ibid., 211.

[168] Ibid., 165.

However, the resultant "Truman Doctrine" was a "blank check."[169] Truman universalized America's support to "free peoples" and provided no context of vital national interest in order to prioritize or constrain the ends to the means available. Contrary to Kennan's intent, the administration also expanded the primary means beyond "economic and financial aid" to a more military-centric strategy. Paul Nitze, Kennan's replacement on the State Department's Policy Planning Staff, authored the National Security Council memorandum 68 (NSC 68), which served as the blueprint for the expansion and "militarization of containment."[170]

The strategy of NSC 68 called for a massive military buildup in order to address the strategic risks posed by the Soviet threat. The American homeland was no longer safe from the Soviet threat due to the "advent of long-range bombers and missiles" and nuclear bombs. NSC 68 acknowledged that appeasement would not work with Stalin any more than it did with Hitler. Thus, "resistance had to be backed by superior force," since power was the only thing that "all dictators understood" and respected.[171] However, there was "considerable opposition to the level of spending that appeared to be required by NSC-68" to build a force capable of balancing Soviet military capability.[172]

The communist North Korean invasion of the Republic of Korea on 24 Jun 1950, "made the threat assessments of NSC-68 seem more realistic, and helped forge a consensus within the administration in support of the NSC-68 programs."[173] The Korean

---

[169] Ibid., 164.

[170] Nelson S. Drew, ed. *NSC-68: Forging the Strategy of Containment* (Washington, DC: National Defense University, 1996), 5, http://www.ou.edu/cls/online/lstd5790security/pdfs/NSC68.pdf (accessed 12 Sep 2011).

[171] McDougall, *Promised Land, Crusader State,* 165.

[172] Drew, 98.

[173] Ibid.

War galvanized the government to commit the nation to the military buildup called for in NSC 68 to prosecute the Cold War. Truman declared a state of "national emergency" to intervene in Korea as the "leaders of the free world," because the "future of civilization depends on what we do."[174] Ultimately, the Korean War—a "police action under the United Nations"—was successful as a limited military campaign because it prevented communist domination of the Korean peninsula and restored the status quo before the invasion.[175] More importantly from a strategic perspective, the United States had established a more credible defensive posture in Asia to prevent Soviet control of the industrial might of Japan. However, there was still a flaw in the strategic logic because the *ends* and the *means* were not balanced. The strategy of Containment was in danger of being an *invalid* strategy because it was designed to be a long-term *feasible* strategy that the United States was capable of sustaining.

During his administration, President Eisenhower worked to balance the strategic *ends* and *means* to ensure the long-term *feasibility* of the Containment strategy. Eisenhower devoted his presidency to solving the "Great Equation: balancing requisite military strength with healthy economic growth" in order to sustain a "reasonable and respectable posture of defense" without "bankrupting the nation."[176] He was committed to impose checks and balances to Truman's "blank check", because he knew the "the only way the United States could lose the Cold War was by militarizing its society, bankrupting its treasury, and exhausting Americans' will to resist."[177]

---

[174] Ibid., 128.

[175] McDougall, *The Constitutional History of U.S. Foreign Policy*, 30.

[176] Robert R. Bowie and Richard H. Immerman. *Waging Peace: How Eisenhower Shaped an Enduring Cold War Strategy* (Oxford: Oxford University Press, 1997), 98.

[177] McDougall, *Promised Land, Crusader State,* 170.

Based on personal experience with Stalin, Eisenhower "did not accept the view of NSC 68" and challenged the strategic *assumptions*, as well as the strategic disparity between the *ends* and *means* in order to develop a *valid* Containment strategy.[178] He discounted the prevailing view of a "Kremlin design for world domination." His reasons were very simple: "The very fact that those men, by their own design, are in the Kremlin, means that they love power….Whenever they start a war, they are taking a great risk of losing that power….And those men in the politburo know that."[179] In response, he understood the critical "need to maintain balance in and among national programs" to maximize strategic effectiveness, but minimize the economic impact to the United States. The U.S. was facing large budgetary deficits, but the "conventional forces of the United States and NATO still remained well below the goal projected for a secure Europe."[180] Despite the entrenched position of the more offensive NSC 68, he launched the Solarium exercise to balance the strategy. The resulting Eisenhower-Dulles New Look (NSC 162/2) laid the groundwork for a sustainable defensive role in support of vital national interests. Eisenhower redefined the West's role, which was to "sustain resistance to Soviet control" until it "can be gradually weakened and loosened from within."[181] NSC 162/2 rebalanced the strategic logic—ends, ways, and means—of Containment, which, established a *feasible* long-term strategy that would serve as the foundation for continued modification of the U.S. Cold War Containment strategy over the next 40 years.

---

[178] Bowie, 247.

[179] Ibid.

[180] Ibid., 245.

[181] Ibid., 249.

Despite the focus on European alliances and economic recovery, Asia was also strategically important to the U.S. Containment strategy. NSC 162/2 stated: "The United States should stress assistance in developing Japan as a major element of strength" and "continue to develop the defensive capacity of Korea and Southeast Asia."[182] Japan was the sole industrial power in Asia. Thus, Japan was the "most important prize in the Far East" and the centerpiece of U.S. strategy in Asia.[183] U.S. Containment strategy demanded that Japan be protected and defended, because to do otherwise risked Japan becoming the "Soviets' workshop of war."[184] This strategy was extremely difficult to execute because of the complex interaction in the region.

In the execution of the Containment strategy, the United States became increasingly embroiled in Asia in order to balance the growing influence and control of the Communist Chinese and Soviets in the region. Japan's economic recovery and regional leadership after World War II was restricted because the traditional trade relationships with South and Southeast Asia were constrained by communist influence and control of much of the region, as well as the "communist led insurrection in Indochina."[185] According to NSC 162/2, Indochina's strategic importance was driven by the requirement to contain the spread of communism and carve out a viable trading block for the economic recovery of Asia, which "probably would compel the United States to react with military force either locally at the point of attack or generally against the military power of the aggressor." The U.S. supported the "principle of collective security

---

[182] U.S. National Security Council. *A Report to the National Security Council: NSC Memorandum 162/2, 30 October 1953*, 21, http://www.fas.org/irp/offdocs/nsc-hst/nsc-162-2.pdf (accessed September 12, 2011)

[183] Bowie, 215.

[184] Ibid.

[185] Ibid., 215-16.

through the United Nations…as a deterrent to continued piecemeal aggression and a promise of an eventual effective world security system."[186] However, the U.S. strategy for collective security in the Far East required the "revival of the economic and military strength of Japan."[187] Unfortunately, this was unacceptable to the pro-Western Nationalistic Chinese and South Korean governments, who suspiciously viewed the U.S. goals for Japan as the "restoration of Japan's lost colonial empire."[188] Therefore, Asia had no sense of cohesion to build "collaborative arrangements" of collective security or trade relationship, so the U.S. was forced to assume the leading role in Asia, which centered on military assistance and economic aid.[189]

The U.S. became increasingly engaged in military assistance to Vietnam when French colonial assistance in Indochina collapsed due to increasing pressure from a determined communist insurgency. Ultimately, the United States fought a protracted war in the jungles of Vietnam to protect and reform the Republic of South Vietnam. However, unlike Korea, the Vietnam War was fought as a progressive war that went beyond a traditional military defense called for in the strategy of Containment. Therefore, the Vietnam War will be analyzed in the next section on Global Meliorism.

Unlike the progressive foreign policy traditions, Containment remained true to the *spirit* of America's foundational foreign policy traditions and served as an effective grand strategy during the Cold War. Containment pursued an active and aggressive defense of

---

[186] U.S. National Security Council. *A Report to the National Security Council: NSC Memorandum 162/2*, 9.

[187] Ibid., 11.

[188] Bowie, 216.

[189] Ibid., 216-17.

Liberty, which was "under siege at home and abroad."[190] The strategy was also based on

Washington's edict to maintain a "respectable defense posture" through an active and

collective defense against an aggressive empire. If America and the rest of the "West

remained strong and united, the Soviet empire would sooner or later collapse under its

own contradictions."[191] The United States pursued the collective defense of the West and

Asia, particularly Japan, through NATO and other bilateral defense pacts. Though

Containment utilized a multilateral approach, the U.S. maintained the spirit of

Unilateralism. Despite commitments and alliances across the globe, the United States led

and enforced these alliances, which enhanced and extended national power and influence,

and bolstered America's defensive posture to pursue national interests more effectively.

These alliances were not "entangling" in the traditional sense because they did not restrict

America's "freedom of action" the way an alliance with Britain or France would have in

the 1800s.[192] Containment also extended the protective umbrella of the American System

through "the projection of U.S. military power across the oceans, which made parts of

Asia and the Middle East into virtual protectorates" in order to prevent external

communist coercion and aggression.[193] Likewise, Containment continued the tradition of

Expansionism by securing free access to the global commons to keep trade and resources

flowing throughout the world.[194] Ultimately, Containment served America's vital

---

[190] McDougall, *Promised Land, Crusader State,* 167.

[191] Ibid., 211.

[192] Ibid., 167. Washington's injunction against "entangling alliances" with Britain or France in the 1800s was to prevent the U.S. from being drawn into a war based on British or French national interests, but contrary to American national interests. These collective and bilateral defense agreements pooled national resources and military defense capability to balance and defend against the Soviet and Chinese commnuists, which was in accordance with American national interests.

[193] Ibid., 212.

[194] Ibid.

national interests by counterbalancing Soviet power to ensure that "no hegemonic behemoth" was allowed to "dominate Europe or East Asia."[195] Containment endured because it was *feasible*. Containment was *effective* because it was *realistic* and operated on the same fundamental *assumptions* and strategies used by the Founding Fathers to design the Constitution and develop America's foundational foreign policy traditions.

The U.S. intervened to "block Communism in Greece, Turkey and Korea" in the spirit of Containment, but without the idealistic progressive policies demanding "model democracies" or "revolutionary economic reforms."[196] However, the same flawed progressive assumptions and strategic logic that fueled Progressive Imperialism and Wilsonianism/Liberal Internationalism continued as a strong national strategic undercurrent that competed with the Containment strategy during the Cold War. This duality is evident in the strategy for the Vietnam War, because the strategy focused more on democratizing this sovereign nation, than effectively defending the Republic of South Vietnam against communist aggression. The American strategy to democratize the world would eventually emerge as a new foreign policy tradition—Global Meliorism.

Global Meliorism

Walter McDougall defines Global Meliorism as the "socio-economic and politico-cultural expression of an American mission to make the world a better place." In other words, it is the American mission to take American Liberty to the world. Global Meliorism pushes America's mission beyond Progressive Imperialism or Liberal Internationalism. The export of American Liberty was limited to new territories and

---

[195] Ibid., 210.

[196] Ibid., 187-88.

colonies in Progressive Imperialism. Wilson's vision was to "make the world safe for democracy; Global Meliorists aim to make the world democratic."[197]

Based on the same ideological roots as the Progressive Movement, Walter McDougall traces much of the Global Meliorism tradition back to the Social Gospel movement.[198] The Protestant church played a similar role in early developmental aid programs, just as it did in early American political development through congregational governments and covenants. Large-scale mission projects mobilized "thousands of clerics, spouses, and assistants," as well as, "tens of millions of *donated* dollars" by the late 1800s—establishing a template for the foreign "government aid projects of the mid-twentieth century."[199] In 1819, the American Board of Foreign Missions authorized a mission to proselytize the Sandwich Islands (Hawaii). Their mission was to plant fields and build homes, schools and churches in order to lift the "whole people to an elevated state of Christian civilization" and they "succeeded in Americanizing Hawaii in a matter of two decades."[200] In response to events in Hawaii, a "New Mission Policy" in 1845 opposed "exporting specific Western modes even for the purposes of *social amelioration*," so that missionaries could focus on preaching Christianity in the context of the local culture instead of pushing for cultural assimilation as well.

Despite these lessons, the Social Gospel movement continued unabated with developmental aid and cultural assimilation during the period of Progressive Imperialism.[201] After World War I, American missions continued social reform

---

[197] Ibid., 174.

[198] Ibid.

[199] Ibid., 174-75.

[200] Ibid., 174.

[201] Ibid., 175.

programs "directly attuned to human needs." Under the leadership of men like John D. Rockefeller, Jr., missionaries became the "Peace Corps types before the Peace Corps."[202] Herbert Hoover also played a large role in converting American charity into official U.S. foreign policy. He believed that developmental aid prevented the "poverty, injustice and despair" that caused "revolutions such as those in Mexico, China, and Russia."[203] President Wilson agreed and harnessed Hoover's humanitarian talents as Director, American Relief Administration, which was the precursor to the Post World War II, United Nations Relief and Rehabilitation Administration. After World War II, President Roosevelt committed to a government-funded campaign to rebuild the "postwar world" through international organizations such as the International Monetary Fund and the World Bank.[204]

The successful means utilized after World War II—the Marshall Plan and the reconstruction of Germany and Japan—are often used in the arguments for the universal effectiveness of the Global Meliorist tradition, but the reality is much more complex.[205] Germany and Japan certainly do not represent a standard template. First of all, the United States is unlikely to commit to that level of intervention again—national mobilization to conquer a country and a full-scale occupation with decades of development and billions of dollars of aid. The American people are even less likely to accept the sacrifices required to succeed. Second, the United States and her allies did not have to develop an industrial infrastructure in Germany or Japan because they were both

---

[202] Ibid.

[203] Ibid., 176.

[204] Ibid., 177.

[205] Ibid., 209-10.

highly developed nations. Third, the Europeans themselves played a major role in Germany's development. Evidence of this fact is that Europeans provided "80 percent of the capital invested in those years," which would indicate that the Marshall Plan was not an "economic miracle," but rather facilitated the engagement and "integration of Western Europe."[206] The last point is that it was ultimately the German people themselves who created a "more democratic and peaceable country," and it was the Japanese people who worked to "reform and recast Japan into a peaceful and democratic nation."[207] True development and self-government must come from the people themselves. Otherwise, it will not endure.

Despite these unique conditions and factors that led to success in these developed nations, many viewed the developmental aid concept as universally applicable. However, the undeveloped Third World nations that Global Meliorists targeted for development were very different than Germany and Japan. The Marshall Plan was designed to rebuild an existing industrial infrastructure, reenergize a highly technical workforce and revive an industrialized economy not for Third World development. Building the infrastructure, educating a workforce, and developing a diversified industry and economy are much more complex problems. These problems become even more difficult if the government itself is neither stable nor supportive of these unrealistic goals.

However, the Truman administration was convinced "that developing nations receiving adequate assistance from the West in the form of planning and technology would aspire to emulate western ideas and would be less vulnerable to Communist

---

[206] Ibid., 180.

[207] Ibid., 178-79.

agendas."[208] In his 1949 inaugural address, Truman offered the Point Four program for developing nations—patterned after his progressive New Deal programs. The political and economic concepts may have been foreign to the Asian nations, but they were certainly willing to accept economic aid. Thirty-four countries signed up for Truman's Point Four developmental agreements at a cost of $156 million a year. Though these development efforts showed some signs of progress, Harvard economist John Galbraith alluded that the U.S. must do even more: "Above and far beyond Point Four, we must put ourselves on the side of truly popular government with whatever pressure we can properly employ."[209] However, the proper limit of this pressure was stretched beyond acceptable limits of American Liberty in Vietnam, where the first Global Meliorist war was supposedly designed to reform the nation and create a popular democratic government where it had never existed.

The Vietnam War: A War of Global Meliorism

The logic of the Kennedy administration's *strategy* in Vietnam was invalidated by false assumptions and dogmatic ideology. The strategic ends were not realistic from the beginning. The administration believed that "a Communist victory in Vietnam would signal the Communist powers and entire third World that insurgencies work and Western

---

[208] Ibid., 181.

[209] John Kenneth Galbraith, "Making 'Point 4' Work: Some Unsolved Problems in Aiding Backward Areas," *Commentary* (September 1950): 229, quoted in Library of Congress, *Technical information for Congress: Report to the Subcommittee on Science, Research and Technology of the Committee on Science and Technology, U.S. House of Representatives, Ninety-sixth Congress, first session.* 3d ed. (Washington: U.S. Government Printing Office, 1979), 95-6, Hathitrust Digital Library, http://hdl.handle.net/2027/mdp.39015081271119 (accessed May 25, 2012). "During the war a new and damaging phrase, 'American know-how,' entered our vocabulary….For many the charm of Point 4 was the notion that we could deliver this know-how by the planeload to every corner of the world at little cost to ourselves." Another mistake was trying to convert or destroy their cultures in the process of introoducing technology and developing civilization via a form of Americanization.

development strategies don't."[210] Therefore, Vietnam became the proving ground for the

United States to demonstrate that Western development and democracy were

economically and politically superior to Communism. In 1961, National Security Action

Memorandum 52 stated that the official U.S. objectives in Vietnam were "to prevent

Communist domination of South Vietnam" and create "a viable and increasingly

democratic society."[211] Thus, Vietnam became a line in the sand in the ideological Cold

War with Communism.   However, the administration's unrealistic strategic end created

an insurmountable strategic dilemma.

Strategic tension developed between defeating the military threat and the political

reforms needed to create a more democratic society. Henry Kissinger pinpointed the

essential tension in the strategic logic: "the central dilemma became that America's goal

of introducing a stable democracy in South Vietnam could not be attained in time to head

off a guerilla victory, which was America's strategic goal. America would have to

modify either its military or its political objectives."[212] The reality of the strategic

environment presented a strategic risk that demanded a realignment of ends, ways, and

means to make the strategy effective. However, the Kennedy/Johnson administration

rejected a more traditional Containment military intervention similar to Korea.[213]

Colonel Harry Summers also criticizes the strategy in Vietnam versus Korea in his book,

On Strategy: A Critical Analysis of the Vietnam War: "Instead of concentrating our

---

[210] McDougall, *Promised Land, Crusader State*, 187.

[211] U.S. President. The White House. *National Security Action Memorandum No. 52 (NSAM 52)*. John F. Kennedy Presential Library and Museum. National Security Action Memoranda. Document images from the Presidential Papers of John Fitzgerald Kennedy, National Security Files. http://www.jfklibrary.org/Asset-Viewer/KDit5FSwHEmiuwttNVhDZQ.aspx (accessed March 1, 2012).

[212] Henry A. Kissinger, *Diplomacy* (New York: Simon and Schuster, 1994), 649.

[213] McDougall, *Promised Land, Crusader State*, 187-88.

efforts on repelling external aggression as we had done in Korea we also took upon ourselves the task of nation building...an error we never made in Korea."[214] Ultimately, the result was the failure of America to achieve either the military or the political objective.

The Vietnam strategy also departed from the traditional American political concepts of popular sovereignty, which proved counterproductive to the ultimate objectives of the war. Lyndon Johnson proclaimed in 1966 his "overriding rule" in the context of Vietnam: "Our foreign policy must always be an extension of this Nation's domestic policy. Our safest guide to what we do abroad is always take a good look at what we are doing at home."[215] However, this drove an *unacceptable* strategy to use American *foreign* policy to shape South Vietnam's *domestic* policy. The reality in Vietnam was that the consent of the corrupt government in Saigon was not the same thing as the consent of the South Vietnamese people. Americans were fighting to convince the people of the legitimacy of the regime in Saigon, which was largely viewed by the people as corrupt and illegitimate, because they seemed to be more interested in staying in power than governing for the good of the people. For example, South Vietnamese rulers were reluctant to pursue rural land reform because they could not afford to lose the support and power base of the "landlord class" and risk having to "confront an empowered

---

[214] Harry G. Summers, Jr., *On Strategy: A Critical Analysis of the Vietnam War* (New York: Dell, 1984), 229.

[215] Lyndon B. Johnson, *Lyndon B. Johnson: 1966 (In Two Books): Containing the Public Messages, Speeches, and Statements of the President.* Book II—July 1 to December 31, 1966 (Washington: United States Government Printing Office, 1967), 908. Hathitrust Digital Library. http://hdl.handle.net/2027/miua.4731549.1966.002 (accessed May 25, 2012).

peasantry."[216] Despite these inconsistencies, the United States worked tirelessly to create legitimacy and progress through the development effort.

Unfortunately, the developmental strategy for Vietnam relied on unproven progressive theories developed and executed by social scientists without mitigating the risk of exporting them for use in this high-stakes ideological war. Armed with a "surfeit of theories regarding the economic development of the Third World," McNamara confidently—if not arrogantly—executed a "comprehensive effort involving political, economic, and ideological measures as well as military" in what has been termed a "social scientists' war" in Vietnam.[217] By 1966, Vietnam was receiving "43 percent of the worldwide USAID funding" with little positive results, since "South Vietnam's cities—like much of inner-city America—soon became corrupt and dependent welfare zones," each with an associated "black market."[218] Unfortunately, this is one of the critiques of developmental aid and the associated social programs because it actually fuels corruption in the government receiving aid. There seems to be a "contradiction inherent in programs whose purpose is to demonstrate the superiority of the free market model but whose methods are entirely statist [centrally controlled by the state]…thereby subsidizing socialism at best and corruption at worst."[219]

Ultimately, the Global Meliorist strategy in Vietnam was ineffective because of *unrealistic ends* with *hidden risk* based on *flawed assumptions*. It is unrealistic to expect

---

[216] McDougall, *Promised Land, Crusader State,* 192.

[217] Ibid., 189.

[218] Ibid., 193.

[219] Ibid., 209. In 1996, the London School of Economics conducted a comprehensive study on foreign aid in ninety-two developing nations and determined that "no relationship exists between the levels of aid and rates of growth in the recipient countries," but it has "tended to discourage the lowering of tax rates and other barriers to investment and growth in the target countries,while 'increasing the size of recipient governments and lining the pockets of elites.'"

that the United States can transform a nation governed by a corrupt and strong centralized

government into an increasingly democratic society. The country was lacking a cohesive

national community or a true representative self-government and there was little national

unity between tribes and ethnic groups. The nation was further divided by an ongoing

Communist insurgency. The conditions in South Vietnam were not conducive to the

grass roots development of a democratic society. Additionally, South Vietnam's leaders

were simply not going to relinquish power, in accordance with human nature, nor would

it have been safe to do so in the face of an insurgency. Installing a democracy in

Vietnam would have been like opening Pandora's Box. All of the divisive forces that the

strong central government controlled to maintain civil order would have been unleashed,

causing chaos and civil disorder that the Communists would have easily exploited.

The strategy was also *invalid* because the coercive means used in Vietnam to

export the American model did not pass the *acceptability* test.[220] The ends did not justify

the means. The United States tried to justify these means by exporting their own

domestic policy—how it takes care of its own people—as foreign policy. This

progressive strategy seems to epitomize the Golden Rule: "Do unto others as you would

have them do unto you." However, one nation's *foreign* policy forced on another

nation's *domestic* policy without the *consent* of that nation's people represents the very

essence of *tyranny*. Colonel Harry Summers confirms this strategic error. Vietnam was

"the international version of our domestic Great Society programs where we *presumed*

that we knew what was best for the world in terms of social, political, and economic

---

[220] This strategy did not pass the other tests of validity either, but the acceptibility test is the most significant. The suitability test failed because the ways and means were ineffective to achieve the ends, particularly since they were unrealistic. The feasibility test failed because the level of intervention, support, funding and national will could not be sustained to achieve the strategic ends.

development and saw it as our duty to *force* the world into the American mold—to act

not so much as the World's Policeman as the World's Nanny."[221] Ultimately, coercion or

force is not the pathway for true civil liberty and long-term civil order. Simply stated,

nations cannot be converted to a true democratic society by coercion or force, because

true consent cannot coexist with coercion, and without consent, true popular sovereignty

cannot exist.

Despite the failures and strategic shortfalls of Global Meliorism in the

undeveloped world—as evidenced in Vietnam—the tradition is still an active foreign

policy in the United States. President Clinton capitalized on the end of the Cold War as

an opportunity to continue to pursue Global Meliorism via both developmental and

military means.[222] The military means of coercion and force of this strategy remain

unacceptable to American Liberty. However, the Global Meliorism tradition—expressed

again in neo-conservatism—guided President George W. Bush's unrealistic objectives of

establishing stable democracies in Afghanistan and Iraq after the military campaigns

conquered the countries and replaced the governments. According to the 2006 National

Security Strategy, Global Meliorism was still a core foreign policy tradition in American

grand strategy:

> It is the policy of the United States to seek and support democratic
> movements and institutions in every nation and culture, with the ultimate
> goal of ending tyranny in our world. In the world today, the fundamental
> character of regimes matters as much as the distribution of power among
> them. The goal of our statecraft is to help create a world of democratic,
> well-governed states that can meet the needs of their citizens and conduct

---

[221] Summers, 229.

[222] McDougall, *Promised Land, Crusader State,* 198.

themselves responsibly in the international system. This is the best way to provide enduring security for the American people.[223]

In pursuit of this strategy, America has "stood for the spread of democracy in the broader Middle East" and "aided a new, democratic government to rise in its place," by fighting two long protracted wars after the swift military defeat of two despotic regimes.[224] Many of the same strategic lessons of Vietnam directly apply to Iraq and Afghanistan. Ultimately, the Progressive Imperialism, Wilsonianism and Global Meliorism are all based on *flawed assumptions* that introduce *hidden risks* and *invalid strategies*, which are both associated with progressivism.

Historical Criticism of America's Modern Foreign Policy Traditions

As demonstrated, the foreign policy traditions established by the Founding Fathers were generally effective, but the modern progressive traditions were much less effective due to significant strategic risk introduced by these strategies. These traditions provide little success or credible evidence to abandon the wisdom and judgment of the men who shaped the U.S. Constitutions and the foreign policy traditions that have established the foundation of American grand strategy. The progressive foreign policy traditions—Progressive Imperialism, Wilsonianism/Liberal Internationalism, and Global Meliorism—are founded on different strategic assumptions, which are fundamentally flawed. *Strategic assumptions* are insidious, because unrealistic assumptions typically lead to *unrealistic strategic ends*, which lead to *invalid strategies* and introduce significant *strategic risk*—risk that is usually not apparent. Flawed assumptions make it

---

[223] U.S. President, *National Security Strategy* (Washington DC: Government Printing Office, March 2006), 1.

[224] Ibid., i.

difficult for the decision makers to make informed strategic decisions because of the hidden risk imbedded in the strategy. Historically, these hidden risks have resulted in significant strategic consequences, though the reasons may not have been immediately apparent at the time.

Flawed Assumptions and Hidden Risks

The United States accepted significant hidden risk in the three progressive foreign policy traditions of American grand strategy based on the following fundamentally *flawed assumptions*. The first assumption is that human nature is perfectible. The second assumes that the spread of democracies or republics would prevent war or usher in a more utopian state of world peace. The third presumes that an international "League" of United Nations can eliminate war or usher in a utopian state of world peace.

The first flawed assumption is the *perfectibility of human nature*. However, the unchanging *depravity*—not the perfectibility—of human nature, was a central truth and fundamental assumption used in the design of the U.S. Constitution, as well as the first four foreign policy traditions. The progressive traditions that followed were founded on the *perfectibility* of human nature. This is a fundamental shift in a foundational assumption. Ironically, if any situation warranted an idealistic outlook on human nature it should have been the ideal conditions presented in the homogeneous and religious nature of the Anglo-Protestant Christian community in America. However, despite these ideal conditions, the depravity of human nature constitutes *the* foundational assumption that the Founding Fathers used to design the governmental institutions in the Constitution, based on personal experiences and the lessons of history.

The Founding Fathers sought to mitigate the *depravity of human nature* in the

innovative design of government in the Constitution. The only effective mitigation

strategy was to pit men against men, ambition against ambition, and power against

power. *The Federalist Papers* declares this truth and the requirement for the separation,

checks and balances on power in order to mitigate human nature via the institutional

design of government in the Constitution.

> It may be a reflection on human nature that such devices should be
> necessary to control the abuses of government. But what is government
> itself but the greatest of all reflections on human nature? If men were
> angels, no government would be necessary. If angels were to govern men,
> neither external nor internal controls on government would be necessary.
> In framing a government which is to be administered by men over men,
> the great difficulty lies in this: you must first enable the government to
> control the governed; and in the next place oblige it to control
> itself…experience has taught mankind the necessity of auxiliary
> precautions.[225]

Hence, the Constitution mitigated this risk through the innovative institutional systems to

separate, check, and balance the branches of government in order to prevent any

individual or faction from usurping the power of government to oppress the people.

A theory can easily make bold predictions of the effectiveness and expected

success based on an idealistic assumption of the *perfectibility of human nature*. This

assumption is based on the belief that the continuing civilization or evolution of humans

leads inevitably towards perfection. Virtually all idealistic or utopian political theories

must rely on this false assumption in order for the theory to be valid. The strategic logic

may be sound, but the false assumption invalidates the strategy in the same way that a

false assumption invalidates a logical argument. The reality of the strategic environment

exposes the real nature of the risk. Therefore, when this theoretical assumption is

---

[225] Hamilton, Madison, and Jay, 318.

confronted with the reality of human nature, the strategic risk becomes strategic consequences. The critical point to remember is that a strategic end based on an idealistic assumption may be unachievable, regardless of the amount of blood and treasure sacrificed to achieve it.

In contrast, the Founding Fathers designed both the Constitution and the first four traditions on the presumptive truth of the depravity of man.[226] All of the first four foreign policy traditions were established by Presidents who were also Founding Fathers—Washington, Adams, Jefferson, Madison, and Monroe. Therefore, these traditions were founded on the same principles as the U.S. Constitution. This at least partially accounts for the long-term effectiveness of the Constitution and the first four foreign policy traditions versus the strategic risks and consequences generated by the more modern progressive traditions.

The second flawed assumption that characterizes America's more modern foreign policy traditions, particularly Progressive Imperialism and Global Meliorism, is that the spread of democracies or republics will prevent war or usher in a utopian state of world peace. Though it is anecdotally true that modern liberal democracies have not gone to war in modern history, there seems to be a simple reason. Since World War I, the "free world" has been united against a virtually unbroken string of common enemies—fascism, communism and terrorism—in order to defeat these threats and secure vital national interests. The historical record indicates that competing interests could lead to conflict within the "free world" once free from a common enemy or threat. The Founding Fathers

---

[226] Washington, *The Writings of George Washington from the original Manuscript Sources, 1745-1799*, Vol 10, 363. "It is vain to exclaim against the depravity of human nature on this account; the fact is so, the experience of every age and nation proved it and we must in great measure, change the constitution of man, before we can make it otherwise. No institution, not built on the presumptive truth of these maxims can succeed."

were keenly aware of the war-torn history of past democracies and republics and they developed the Constitution to mitigate these pitfalls through the creation of a "more perfect Union."

The historical record indicates that the form of government does not prevent conflict or predispose nations to war. Instead, war is driven by the depraved nature of man, since human nature is the common driver across all polities and governments. In the justification for the Constitution, Alexander Hamilton devotes an entire article of *The Federalist Papers* to illustrate the impacts that human nature would have on their country if they chose to reject the Constitution and remained a loose and ineffective confederation of sovereign states under the Articles of Confederation:

> A man must be far gone in Utopian speculations who can seriously doubt that if these States should either be wholly disunited, or only united in partial confederacies...would have *frequent and violent contests with each other*. To presume a want of motives for such contests as an argument against their existence would be to forget that men are ambitious, vindictive, and rapacious. To look for a continuation of harmony between a number of independent, unconnected sovereignties situated in the same neighborhood would be to disregard the uniform course of human events, and to set at defiance the accumulated experience of the ages....Let experience, the least fallible guide of human opinions, be appealed to for an answer.[227]

Based on the lessons of history, Hamilton describes the violent contests and war that characterized the experience of the previous republics of Sparta, Athens, Rome, Carthage, Venice and Holland. He then concludes: "There have been, if I may so express it, almost as many popular as royal wars."[228] Therefore, a democracy or republic is not immune to war, even with each other because human nature ultimately drives wars.

---

[227] Hamilton, Madison, and Jay, 48.

[228] Ibid., 48-52

The American experience also confirms this historical truth. The unity and liberty harnessed by the Constitution did not prevent war in the United States. Despite the carefully crafted constitutional check on human nature and the sovereign power of the states within America's great Republic, it was still torn apart by the Civil War—just as Hamilton predicted. Despite America's democratic principles of Liberty, the Union and the Confederacy still engaged in a brutal war similar to the other competing republics of history, once the southern states seceded to form a separate, competing confederate republic. Therefore, there is little credible evidence in history or experience that supports the assumption that the spread of democracies or republics would prevent war or usher in a utopian state of world peace.

The third flawed assumption that characterizes America's more modern foreign policy traditions, especially Wilsonianism/Liberal Internationalism, is that an international League of United Nations can eliminate war or usher in a utopian state of world peace. Once again, human nature is a driving factor. Immanuel Kant confirms human nature's role in international relations: "The *depravity of human nature* shows itself without disguise in the *unrestrained relations of nations* to each other, while in the law-governed civil state much of this is hidden by the *check of government.*"[229] The nations of the world would certainly benefit from a true "check of government," which would enforce the rule of international law and govern international relations. However, a true international or supra-national world government does not exist.

The current United Nations Charter constitutes a loose international *assembly* of nations, not a supra-national world government or even a true international *community*

_____

[229] Immanuel Kant, *Perpetual Peace: A Philosophical Essay, 1795,* trans.by M. Campbell Smith (New York: The MacMillan Company, 1917), 131, http://files.libertyfund.org/files/357/0075_Bk.pdf (accessed 12 September, 2011).

united by consensual common interests, values and rights. Certainly, there are no legitimate government institutions that have been granted sovereignty or power over the nations to check international actions. The United Nations has not been granted sovereignty or authority in accordance with popular sovereignty nor are the institutional mechanisms effectively designed to check human nature. In fact, the United Nations Charter grants even less authority and power to the United Nations than the sovereign states granted to the ineffective federal government in the Articles of Confederation. Therefore, there is no supra-national government to either check or compel the sovereign nations, which means that international relation remain largely unrestrained. Sovereign nations must then protect themselves and promote and secure their own vital interests in the only way that nations can once diplomatic and other peaceful options are exhausted—war or the threat of war.

Despite being ineffective as a true supra-national government, the United Nations is effective as a broad international forum to foster consensus on specific issues to improve international relations, albeit with limited results. Similar to the states under the Articles of Confederation, each sovereign nation under the current United Nations Charter still has the freedom to choose whether they will support proposed policies or provide forces to enforce any resolutions, based on their own national interests. When the sovereign nations agree, particularly the members of the Security Council, the U.N. is generally effective. However, when they do not, the U.N. is not generally effective. Competing national interests dictate international gridlock similar to the problems the Founding Fathers faced with the Articles of Confederation. Therefore, the United Nations is incapable of providing a foundation for lasting peace in its current form.

Multilateral engagements can still be effective for resolving specific international issues through consensus and temporary coalitions based on focused areas of common interest. However, the *depravity of human nature* and power will still dictate the overall reality of international relations and, thus, war will always be an integral part of the *unrestrained relations* between sovereign nations.

The Federalist Papers proposes a solution that serves as a blueprint for a peaceful and effective solution for an effective government over sovereign nations. The Founding Fathers incorporated this solution in the Constitution to correct the institutional weakness of the Articles of the Confederation by federating the sovereign states under a strong national government with sovereign authority over the people. The same rules of federation apply to nations. Hamilton describes the process: "NEIGHBORING NATIONS…are naturally ENEMIES of each other, unless their common weakness forces them to league in a CONFEDERATE REPUBLIC, and their *constitution* prevents the differences that neighborhood occasions, extinguishing that secret jealousy which disposes all states to aggrandize themselves at the expense of their neighbors."[230] Therefore, federation requires mutual consent of each nation to form a unified community—based on common interests, values and rights—which enables a consolidation of sovereignty to form a government under the same constitution. Of course, this was difficult to achieve in America even under ideal conditions. It would be near impossible to achieve on an international scale with so many divergent and competing interests among the nations of the world.

---

[230] Hamilton, Madison, and Jay, 54.

However, Immanuel Kant proposes a similar, and supposedly practical, mechanism to enable a federal union of nations to expand in the ongoing quest for "perpetual peace."

> The practicability or objective reality of this idea of federation which is to extend gradually over all states and so lead to *perpetual peace* can be shewn. For, if Fortune ordains that a powerful and enlightened people should form a republic—which by its very nature is inclined to perpetual peace—this would serve as a centre of federal union for other states wishing to join, and thus secure conditions of freedom among the states in accordance with the idea of the law of nations. Gradually, through different unions of this kind, the federation would extend further and further.[231]

Of course, the immediate question becomes which republic is worthy to serve as the "centre of federal union for other states." It is unlikely that any established nation today, especially the United States, would sacrifice their constitutional sovereignty to unite with another republic by consent due to the inevitable divergent interests, values and rights. On the other hand, the United States has long since rejected the possible role as the central federal union, since it has been unwilling to annex full-fledged states into the United States since Hawaii became a state. Looking elsewhere, the European Union demonstrates the complex difficulty of this concept. It is true that the European Union has been gradually expanding its union, but the political ties are mostly economic. Even this very limited mechanism to consolidate commercial sovereignty has been severely limited and frustrated by the expected competing national interests of the member nations due to human nature.

Therefore, the concept of a growing worldwide Confederate Republic may seem theoretically possible, but it is not realistic in the context of popular sovereignty and the

---

[231] Kant, 134-35.

depravity of human nature. It is especially idealistic to believe that all nations on earth, will sacrifice their own sovereignty to form a true supra-national government that had sovereign authority and power over all the nations of the world. Even if a coalition of nations, united in a limited international community to form a true confederate republic of nations, this republic would still be in eventual violent competition with any of the nations outside of that republic, even if they too had joined together into a different but competing confederate republic. America's Civil War and the history of wars between republics is certainly evidence of that reality. Therefore, war and the threat of war will still be a prominent feature in international relations. Human nature and competing interests are unavoidable barriers to overcome, which means that "perpetual peace" will remain a "utopian speculation."

Unrealistic Ends and Invalid Strategies

The flawed assumptions and unrealistic ends of the Global Meliorist foreign policy associated with America's mission to spread democracies or republics by coercion or force also suffers from fundamental flaws in the strategic logic, which results in an *invalid strategy*. On the surface, the strategic end to spread republican democracies throughout the world seems a noble and morally virtuous pursuit. The strategic ends are unrealistic and the strategy is not *valid* because the selected means—the military instrument of power—does not meet the tests of *suitability, acceptability* or *feasibility*.[232] This strategy is not *suitable* because unrealistic preconditions are required for the strategy to be effective through the use of the military instrument of power. The strategy is also

---

[232] This criticism focuses strictly on the military means of this mission. The other means—diplomatic, economic or informational instruments of power—are both necessary and remain valid unless incorporated with the use of coercive force, but require a long-term commitment. Likewise the legitimate means of development and aid for foreign countries remains a valid, though not always effective, strategy.

not *acceptable* because the *ends* do not justify the *means*—the militant use of coercive force—in the context of civil liberty and popular sovereignty. The strategy is also not *feasible* because the strategy requires an unsustainable requirement for military resources to continue executing this ineffective strategy.

The military means selected for this strategy are not *suitable* because the means of coercion or force are not effective in the development of a stable constitutional democratic republic based on the principles of popular sovereignty. However, the real issue is the strategic end is *unrealistic*. It is simply not enough for a strategic *end* to be morally justified. The *ends* must be realistic, or the strategy will never be successful because no combination of ways and means will be *suitable* to achieve an *unrealistic end*.

Establishing a constitutional republic was difficult in the United States under ideal conditions. It is unrealistic to expect even favorable conditions in most foreign countries where military forces are being employed. A constitutional democracy or republic is a powerful form of government for unlocking the enormous unified potential of a people with the proper preconditions—a functionally unified community of peoples with common interests, values and rights that is used to self-government. These preconditions rarely exist and cannot be effectively imposed or created externally. A democratic form of government is unpredictable and potentially dangerous if unleashed on a divided nation not accustomed to representative self-government, but well accustomed to the use of violence to resolve conflict. Establishing a stable republican democracy in a nation is much more complex that a conventional military strategy. Concrete goals can still be achieved, but to what effect? Populations can be liberated from tyrannical rule in order to grant them liberty. A constitution can be developed. Elections can be coordinated, scheduled, secured and executed. These are all realistic ends that can be achieved.

However, a national constitution is just a piece of paper unless *the people* respect and

support that constitution. The people must trust the national government the constitution

establishes as legitimate. The stable balance between civil liberty and order that

accompanies true popular sovereignty is more than just temporary freedom from tyranny

combined with a constitution and an election. Ultimately, the people must decide for

themselves to put aside their own diverse interests and differences. The people must

decide to unite themselves together as a people by their own *consent* in order to work out

the difficult task of governing a nation and taking care of the needs of the population.

The reality of human nature makes this strategic end unrealistic, if not

impossible, because of the divisive forces of individual and factional interests, such as

tribes, ethnic and religious groups in most nations where military forces are selected as

the primary means. Therefore, it is an *unrealistic end* and the military means are

unsuitable for achieving the end in accordance with popular sovereignty. The *unrealistic*

ends were certainly a factor in the strategic failure in Vietnam. The unrealistic ends in

Afghanistan and Iraq have also contributed to the limited strategic success.

This strategy is also not *acceptable* because the military *means* and the use of

coercive force are incompatible with civil liberty and popular sovereignty—regardless of

the supposedly moral nature of the end. Popular sovereignty requires that the people

have the freedom to consent, which can only be achieved in the absence of coercion or

force. The very nature of coercion and force violate the principle of popular sovereignty.

Consent must have the freedom to choose without the threat of coercion or force.

Without true consent, there is no community. Without community, there is no legitimate government. Without legitimate government, there is no civil liberty. Without civil liberty, there will be little civil order without tyranny. It is also important to remember that force or coercion does not have to be intended to be felt by the population. Perception is reality. Coercion or force may be solely intended to secure the people, but the presence of force may be coercive in, and of itself. Since, popular sovereignty is based on the consent of the people. The Philippine-American War is a graphic example of the *unacceptable* use of military force to establish a constitutional republic, which was morally justified as a "benevolent assimilation" because the American leadership decided that it would be best for the Filipino people. The Filipino people should have had the freedom to decide what was best for the Filipinos. The ends simply did not justify the means.

In the post-Cold War period, the United States has touted "liberal democracy" as panacea for liberated autocratic nations deeply divided by ethnic, tribal and religious differences, such as Afghanistan and Iraq. In reality, instituting a liberal democracy in a nation that is divided by hostile factions and has no tradition of representative government is like opening Pandora's Box. James Madison stated: "Liberty is to faction what air is to fire."[233] It will certainly require force to secure and control the ensuing chaos. Historically, the result will be the use of tyranny to restore civil order at the expense of civil liberty. Immanuel Kant acknowledges this truth in his 1795 treatise *Perpetual Peace,* by explaining that "experience" trumps the "theoretical idea of perpetual peace" because a divided people with a "diversity of individual wills" can only

---

[233] Hamilton, Madison, and Jay, 73.

be unified "by force."[234] No one can realistically expect that once a powerful ruler has "united a wild multitude into one people, he will leave it to them to bring about a legal constitution by their common will. It amounts to this. *Any ruler who has once got the power in his hands will not let the people dictate laws for him.*"[235] Tyranny and power are usually required to establish order, and rulers will unlikely forfeit that power unless forced to by a greater power. Thus, the cycle of tyranny continues. Therefore, the moral, but unrealistic, strategic end to "create a world of democratic, well governed states," will realistically result in a form of tyranny rather than the true civil liberty and order intended. In this case, the *idealistic intent* of the morally justified, but unrealistic end does not justify the *real consequences* of the use of force or the tyranny that results. Ultimately, both the means and results will likely be *unacceptable*.

This strategy is also not *feasible* because the demand imposed on the military instrument of power requires an unsustainable level of military means to sustain the protracted wars that will likely result from such an ineffective strategy. Americans have never entered a war without the ultimate goal of victory, but the United States seems to have forgotten the true sense of victory in the context of grand strategy. According to Liddell Hart, "Victory in the true sense implies that the state of peace, and of one's people, is better after the war than before. Victory in this sense is only possible if a quick result can be gained or if a *long effort can be economically proportioned to the national resources*. The end must be adjusted to the means."[236] Therefore, true victory in war links directly to the effectiveness of a nation's grand strategy to maintain the long-term

---

[234] Kant, 164.

[235] Ibid, 164-65.

[236] B. H. Liddell Hart, *Strategy* (New York: Penguin Group, 1991), 357.

balance of the ends and means in the continuation of policy. This requires a realistic risk-benefit analysis of the grand strategy *before* the nation is committed to war. However, benefits are often unrealistically elevated and risks minimized in this analysis, which results more often in a costly protracted war versus the "quick result" or "economically proportioned" long effort described above. As an example, a quick result was achieved in the Mexican-American War as a punitive expedition. However, it could have easily progressed to a protracted counter-insurgency campaign. Fortunately, President Polk wisely disregarded the growing popular pressure to annex all of Mexico. Unfortunately, the United States has engaged in a growing list of costly protracted wars, such as the Philippine-American War, the Vietnam War, and, more recently, the wars in Afghanistan and Iraq. These wars were justified with promises of idealistic results, reasonable costs and acceptable risks. Victory was certainly illusive, but it is still unclear if victory was even achievable.

In light of America's protracted wars in Afghanistan and Iraq, Sun Tzu, an ancient Chinese strategist and author of the "first of the martial classics," *The Art of War*, emphatically states a warning that is just as valid in the 21st century as it was some 2500 years ago. "Victory is the main object in war. If this is long delayed, weapons are blunted and morale is depressed. When troops attack cities, their strength will be exhausted. When the army engages in protracted campaigns the resources of the state will not suffice….For there has never been a protracted war from which a country has benefited."[237] Unfortunately, this truth—originally learned by Americans in Vietnam—is being relearned the hard way by yet another generation. Both Afghanistan and Iraq

---

[237] Sun Tzu, *The Art of War,*. trans. Samuel B. Griffith (New York: Oxford University Press, 1971), 73.

began as punitive wars. Unfortunately, after the tyrannical regimes were quickly defeated, they transitioned into a protracted Global Meliorist war with the unrealistic strategic end to establish stable democracies where they have never existed.

Ultimately, historians will decide whether the protracted wars in Afghanistan and Iraq will be considered victories. However, after over a decade of war and the devastating impact to the U.S. economy, any resultant victory in peace that is better than the status quo will be tainted by the costly toll it has taken to secure it. It will certainly be difficult to justify the loss of over 6000 U.S. service members with a total of over 236,000 dead, and estimated costs roughly ranging between $1.4 and $3.7 trillion.[238] These two ongoing protracted wars have certainly taxed, if not strained, a fragile U.S. economy. This is stark evidence that the United States failed to pursue a realistic and *feasible* American grand strategy.

Continuing to pursue the Global Meliorist strategy with the military instrument of power is the ultimate protracted war. When confronted with the realities of *undeveloped* Asia in 1966, Senator Fulbright rightly questioned "the ability of the United States or any other Western nation…to create stability where there is chaos, the will to fight where there is defeatism, democracy where there is no tradition of it, and honest government where corruption is almost a way of life."[239] The Vietnam War proved him correct and the observation seems to be valid across non-western cultures, since human nature is consistent across cultures. Victory has always been the goal, but victory remains out of reach because reality has exposed the true flaws in this strategy through the consequences

---

[238] Daniel Trotto, "Cost of war at least $3.7 trillion and counting," Reuters, New York, Jun 29, 2011 http://www.reuters.com/article/2011/06/29/us-usa-war-idUSTRE75S25320110629 Accessed February 20, 2012.

[239] J. William Fulbright, *The Arrogance of Power* (New York: Random House, 1967), 15.

of flawed assumptions, unrealistic ends, invalid strategies and hidden risks. These lessons must be learned to correct these strategic flaws in American grand strategy. If America continues down this path, it will threaten to militarize society, bankrupt the economy, and jeopardize liberty at home.

In light of the lessons learned from the historical criticism of American grand strategy, it is time for America to return to the solid foundation of the Constitution and the founding foreign policy traditions. Real world experience and the lessons of history must serve as America's guide for human affairs and international relations, not idealistic theories or "Utopian speculations." The United States must return to realistic *assumptions* and *ends*, as well as a *valid* American grand strategy in order to mitigate the strategic risk effectively in the 21st century. Since human nature has not fundamentally changed, Alexander Hamilton's challenge to the American people in *The Federalist Papers* is as true today as it was then.

> Have we not already seen enough of the fallacy and extravagance of those idle theories which have amused us with promises of an exemption from the imperfections, the weaknesses, and the evils incident to society in every shape? Is it not time to awake from the deceitful dream of a golden age and to adopt as a practical maxim for the direction of our political conduct that we, as well as the other inhabitants of the globe, are yet remote from the happy empire of perfect wisdom and perfect virtue?[240]

This historical criticism recommends that America reject the idealistic progressive traditions and return to the realistic foreign policy traditions of the Founding Fathers. **Therefore, the same enduring principles of civil liberty and order that framed America's first grand strategy through the Declaration of Independence, the U.S.**

---

[240] Hamilton, Madison, and Jay, 53.

Constitution and the foreign policy traditions of the Founding Fathers must frame

America's Grand Strategy in the 21st century.

CHAPTER 4: AMERICAN GRAND STRATEGY FOR THE 21ST CENTURY

The development of sound foreign policy for the 21st century requires that the President and Congress continue to build on the foundation established by the U.S. Constitution and the founding foreign policy traditions. Since the flawed assumptions manifest themselves in the modern progressive traditions, there is a requirement to return to the foreign policy traditions of the Founding Fathers in order to reestablish an *effective* American grand strategy. However, though the underlying assumptions and principles are sound, these traditions must be adapted to the new strategic environment to be effective in the 21st century. A reevaluation of American identity is also required to recalibrate American roles and missions. These updates to the original foreign policy traditions will return American grand strategy to the firm foundations established by the Founding Fathers, and effectively address the 21st century strategic environment.

Critical Changes in the Strategic Environment

American grand strategy must also effectively shape and respond to a complex and uncertain strategic environment. Although the depravity of human nature remains a constant, changes in the strategic environment must be addressed to update the four original foreign policy traditions. The following changes encapsulate the critical changes that are most relevant to these foreign policy traditions at the grand strategy level:

1) Globalization and interconnected international trade and commerce have made all nations relative neighbors in the international community.

2) International trade and commerce has always relied on international rights and access to maritime trade routes. However, today, the global commons include a much broader set of domains—air, land, sea, space and cyberspace. Ensuring the

security and continued freedom of access to the global commons constitutes one of the foundations of international order.

3) Weapons of mass destruction, modern transportation, technology and globalization have shrunk the globe and the United States can no longer rely on geographical protection in Fortress America to insulate the nation and the global commons from international and transnational threats. The United States must maintain a respectable and active defense posture in order to secure the homeland, allies and partners against international and transnational aggression. This constitutes another critical foundation of international order.

4) America is faced with more complex threats associated with national, trans-national and environmental threats across multiple globalized domains, which demand multilateral and collective international strategies and solutions to provide the appropriate capabilities and sufficient capacity to balance and counter today's threats.

5) America faces severe fiscal constraints due to an enormous national debt and continuing annual budget deficits that will continue to require significant cuts in government spending as the nation closes out two protracted wars that have been a drain on all of the nation's instruments of power over the last decade. America's power is limited, and the means to respond to the strategic environment are finite. The United States cannot effectively respond to *all* the threats, crises and humanitarian disasters in the world. Therefore, vital national interests must govern American foreign policy and international engagements, if the nation's grand strategy is to remain *feasible*.

The foreign policy traditions of the Founding Fathers be updated to reflect the reality of the strategic environment reflected in these threats and challenges. However, flawed assumptions have driven *unrealistic ends* for American grand strategy. The United States must decide what American grand strategy can realistically achieve in the 21st century. This requires a reevaluation of American identity and the nation's role and mission in the world.

Reevaluating American National Identity

According to Samuel Huntington, the United States has a choice of "three broad concepts" for defining American identity and the nation's corresponding role and mission in the world.[1] These three concepts of American identity are cosmopolitan, imperial, and national. The *cosmopolitan* identity accepts a common identity with the world in such a way that the "world reshapes America" by embracing the world's cultures and peoples in an open society.[2] More importantly, this identity requires that Americans would be governed more by international laws, authorities and organizations—"United Nations, the World Trade Organization, the World Court, customary international law, and global treaties and regimes"—than by traditional state and federal government as established in the Constitution of the United States.[3] The foreign policy tradition of Wilsonianism and Liberal Internationalism partially expressed this identity, albeit with nationalistic caveats. However, the foundation of the cosmopolitan identity rests on the false assumption that there is a world community with consent on: 1) a common international law; and 2) a world government powerful enough to enforce the rule of law in all nations on earth. This identity is also contrary to the supremacy of the U.S. Constitution in the government and identity of the United States. This cosmopolitan identity is contrasted with another option, the imperial identity, which embraces an America that "remakes the world" in the image of America. An *imperial* identity defines American values as universal with a mission to "reshape" the world's "peoples and cultures in terms of American values" with "nation building, humanitarian intervention, and foreign policy as social work."[4] The foreign policy traditions of Progressive Imperialism and Global Meliorism both embrace a form of imperial identity for America. However, the foundation of the

---

[1] Samuel P. Huntington, *Who Are We? The Challenges to America's National Identity* (New York: Simon & Schuster Paperbacks, 2005), 362.

[2] Ibid., 363.

[3] Ibid.

[4] Ibid., 364.

imperial identity rests on additional assumptions or beliefs in: 1) "the supremacy of American power;" and 2) the "universality of American values."[5] American power to reshape the world has definite limits as indicated by the unsuccessful—if not disastrous—results in Vietnam and the challenges faced in Iraq and Afghanistan. It is also apparent that the United States confronts a world that is more accurately defined as multipolar versus the unipolar world that was envisioned to emerge in the post-Cold War period. Nor did the costly long-term commitment in Germany, Japan, Philippines or Korea prove successful in completely Americanizing or reshaping these cultures or peoples in the image of universal American values. In fact, practical experience has proven that the "paradox of democracy" equally gives rise to "anti-American forces," such as "nationalistic populist movements in Latin America" or the "fundamentalist movements in Muslim countries."[6] This negative reaction certainly questions the universality of these values as they are perceived in other nations across the globe. Ultimately, both the cosmopolitan and imperial identities contrast with the *national identity* traditionally defined in America's founding documents.

The traditional *national* identity simply embraces American Liberty and Exceptionalism that has always defined the United States. This includes the unique nature and character of a nation forged by the strong historic core Anglo-Protestant culture, which defined American values and laws and provided the foundation for the Declaration of Independence and the Constitution. The culture today is undeniably more diverse and heterogeneous due to prolific immigration into the American melting pot over the centuries. However, the Founding Fathers designed the Constitution to secure

---

[5] Ibid.

[6] Ibid.

the civil liberty and order of a large, diverse population, but the citizens themselves play a critical role in that process. The protection and guarantee of civil rights for all citizens of the United States was extended to immigrants because they consented to join the national community, embrace American culture, and obey the laws as a true citizen of the United States. The Constitution and the nation's laws continue to secure the blessings of civil liberty in accordance with the principles of popular sovereignty, which have been designed into the institutional system of government in America. Regardless of divergent beliefs and *interests*, citizens of the United States have consented to restrict their *natural liberty* and accepted the *civil responsibility* to obey and submit to the *majority rule* of the national, state and municipal communities based on common *values* and *laws* defined by the majority, which provides the foundation for *civil liberty* and *order* through popular sovereignty. *Popular sovereignty* represents the symbiotic relationship between the *people*, the *community* and the *government*. American citizens continue to have the precious freedom to be diverse and live by different beliefs and *self-interests*, as long as each citizen continues to accept the *civil responsibility* to obey the *laws* for the good of the community. American communities play a critical role in this process because they define *common values*, establish *majority rule*, and secure *civil liberty* for the citizens within the community. In addition, national, state and municipal government *institutions* develop and enforce the *laws* to establish a stable *civil order* in order to protect citizen's *civil rights* and sustain the long-term balance *between liberty and order*. These are the blessings of liberty that American citizens enjoy and should be embraced in the context of a *national identity*.

After the Revolution, the American people originally defined themselves with a *national* identity and the United States should continue to define itself that way. A *national* identity defines America's domestic policy, which secures "the blessings of liberty for ourselves and our posterity." A national identity also defines America's foreign policy by granting other nations the same liberty to choose their own government and way of life without interference or intervention unless that nation acts outside of its borders to threaten or restrict America's national security or freedom at home. Unfortunately, America currently faces an identity crisis that must be resolved. Simply stated, "America cannot become the world and still be America;" likewise, America cannot reshape the world and maintain her own Liberty.[7] America needs to reestablish the foundation of foreign policy back to the traditional *national identity*.

America should return to her foundational national identity, which includes a return to the founding foreign policy traditions—Liberty, Unilateralism, American System, and Expansionism. America should also remain true to the principles of civil liberty and order that have defined the founding documents of the United States for over two centuries. However, in order to be effective in the 21st century, these traditions must be updated to account for the current strategic environment without compromising the traditional foundations or assumptions.

American Foreign Policy Traditions for the 21st Century

Liberty (Exceptionalism)

American Liberty/Exceptionalism must continue to be the foundation of America's grand strategy. It represents the power to unite the nation and defend the

---

[7] Ibid., 365.

liberty of the homeland. However, the United States should be the example of Liberty to the world—the proverbial "City on a Hill" and a beacon of liberty and order—not the "dictatress of the world" that John Quincy Adams warned against. Exceptionalism is just as relevant and important today for Americans as it was to the Founding Fathers. It can also serve as a powerful guide for the aid and development of nations requesting assistance to embrace the foundational principles of liberty based on common interests, values and rights. American Liberty was designed specifically for the United States and besides the example and influence to the world, it was meant to be enjoyed and protected at home. However, this Liberty still represents America's most vital national interest. Exceptionalism remains a warning to the world that Americans will fiercely and zealously defend their Liberty, just as they have done so ably in the past.

However, the foreign policy tradition of Liberty and Exceptionalism does not include or justify a universal mission to Americanize the world. America was never intended to be a revolutionary nation on a militant crusade to proselytize the world with America's way of life or form of government. Power should have little correlation with moral right. In this case, American might does not make it right, nor does a supposedly moral end justify any means. America's great power warrants a timeless warning; America itself is vulnerable to the same corruption of power that is common to all humanity. If America truly believes in the fundamental rights of liberty—freedom of religion, free speech, assembly, the press, and government petition—then other nations should be free to choose their own form of government without being subject to coercion or force. However, each nation will choose a form of government that is uniquely suited to their culture, interests, values and rights. It may not look like the civil liberty/civil order paradigm of the United States because most nations do not possess the same ideal conditions to capitalize on the power of liberty via popular sovereignty as illustrated in the simple equation below.

Civil Liberty = Consenting People + Unified Communities + Representative Govt. = Civil Order

America's situation was ideal for popular sovereignty, but the preconditions that characterized colonial America were unique and certainly not common. Most nations are deeply divided by cultural, ethnic, tribal, religious, racial or other tensions and are characterized more by competing interests, which form conflicting communities rather than a community of unified people. This situation is a recipe for civil disorder with the introduction of liberty and a democratic, representative government as simply expressed in the next equation.

Liberty + Competing People + Conflicting Communities + Representative Govt. = Disorder

This is a stark reminder that liberty is easy to grant, but it is virtually impossible to achieve a true balance of civil liberty and order without the genuine consent and unity of the people, which cannot be forced. In fact, if disorder or chaos results from disunity, a government often finds justification to resort to tyranny or stronger centralized control to establish civil order in the absence or lack of consent and unity.

Coercion and force are still legitimate means to maintain basic *international* order, which includes protecting nations from external coercion and force, protecting and enforcing *international* rights and securing *international* access to the global commons. However, if America chooses coercion and force to shape a nation's *domestic* politics, it no longer serves as an example and instrument of Liberty. Instead, it becomes an instrument of tyranny and an enemy of Liberty.

Unilateralism

Unilateralism should also continue to be a core foreign policy tradition in American grand strategy, albeit with some caveats. It represents the national power of the United States to defend against any threat, as well as deter and defeat any enemy. The United States certainly no longer enjoys the "detached and distant situation" referred to by President George Washington in his Farewell Address. However, much of the wisdom of the "Great Rule" is still applicable to American grand strategy. Globalization has interconnected the world into an international *commercial* community of neighbors. The extension of American "commercial relations" to the rest of the world has certainly played a role in that globalization. However, even in the context of this interconnected commercial community of nations, Washington's warning to maintain as "little *political* connection as possible" still remains valid today.[8] There is still great wisdom in remaining neutral in the internal domestic issues of other nations, whenever possible. Granted, globalization has certainly driven the United States towards more multilateral solutions to global problems, but these solutions should focus on *international* issues rather than interfering in *national domestic* issues.

Additionally, securing vital national interests and international rights requires a unilateral commitment to spend millions for defense in order to maintain a "respectable defensive posture," which includes an active defense.[9] For instance, the fundamental international rights to maritime trade access—one of the foundations for international order—drove America to eventually defend her rights and unilaterally enforce recognized

---

[8] George Washington, "George Washington's Farewell Address, 1796," Avalon Project: Documents in Law, History and Diplomacy, Lillian Goldman Law Library, Yale Law School, http://avalon.law.yale.edu/18th_century/washing.asp (accessed September 20, 2011).

[9] Ibid.

international norms through the Barbary Wars and the War of 1812. International and transnational threats still threaten freedom of access to the Global Commons, which now includes sea, air, space and cyberspace. Although the medium has changed and the threats are much more complex, the same principles that governed American unilateral action in the 1800s still apply today because the threat is, ultimately, still human and driven by human nature. To this end, the United States has extended the nation's military presence throughout the world via regionally oriented geographical combatant commands that are responsible for military engagements in each region. However, rapidly changing asymmetric threats to the Global Commons, such as cyber attack and anti-access, area denial capabilities, require priority attention to ensure sufficient means are available for the United States to effectively counter these asymmetric threats.

Unilateralism also requires an effective means to establish and integrate collective multilateral approaches with unilateral power, without the loss of sovereignty or freedom of action that characterize "entangling alliances" in the international community.[10] As an example, Article 43 of the United Nations Charter explicitly states that U.N. obligations have no sovereign authority over the member nations. Thus, all member actions will be decided and executed by each nation "in accordance with their respective constitutional processes."[11] The 1945 U.N. Participation Act further requires the approval of both houses of Congress to commit U.S. forces to U.N. missions. Therefore, even U.N. participation remains true to Unilateralism and the supremacy of the U.S. Constitution. Ultimately, Washington's "Great Rule" laid down the critical test to guide American Unilateralism. The President and Congress must maintain the freedom of action in

---

[10] Ibid.

[11] McDougall, *The Constitutional History of U.S. Foreign Policy,* 30.

international engagements to "choose peace or war" as "interest guided by justice shall counsel" in accordance with the U.S. Constitution.[12] Multilateral engagement may characterize the strategic approach, but Unilateralism must guide American decisions and actions. This is the true spirit of Unilateralism. It is this spirit, which should guide America's alliances, multilateral engagements, and relationships with international institutions.

American System/Containment

Coupled with Unilateralism, the American System must also continue to be a core foreign policy tradition in American grand strategy. It represents the power to deter and defeat any national or transnational threat, as well as, defend partner nations. The American System has been expanded by an increasingly interconnected international system of treaties and international organizations that center on respect for national sovereignty, while building consensus for collective defense and multilateral action to resolve international problems. For instance, an expansion of the American System characterized the Containment strategy. However, the strategic effect is closer to *checks and balances* or *balancing against* versus containment. The same should be true for the struggle against terrorism and trans-national criminal networks or cyber attacks. The U.S. must balance power against power, humans against humans, networks against networks. Terrorism, trans-national crime or cyber attacks cannot be contained, but military, intelligence, law-enforcement, and even commercial networks can be used as a counter-force to act as a check and balance to resist their movement, progress and expansion.

---

[12] Washington, "George Washington's Farewell Address, 1796."

Possibly, the most succinct—but not complete—expression of the true spirit of American grand strategy outside of the U.S. Constitution is the American System plus the Golden Rule—"Do to others what you would have them do to you."[13] McDougall argues that the foreign policy tradition of Containment during the Cold War represented "extensions of the American System to the opposite shores of the two American Oceans."[14] The intent of the American System was to shield and protect the nations from imperial powers bent on *externally* forcing, coercing, or subverting these nations to adopt a form of government or submit to external control against their consent. However, the United States must not abuse the American System themselves by exerting external force or coercion on these countries to adopt the American form of governance, which occurred in various forms in both the Philippines and Vietnam. Otherwise, the United States becomes just another imperial power willing to use tyranny to exert external political influence and control.

However, the American System does provide for the limited use of force as an international police power as was practiced by the Founding Fathers. Thus, the use of force was limited to international violations that adversely impacted the nation, in accordance with America's vital national interests. This use of military force was integral to the American system from the founding of the country. From 1798 to 1898, the United States deployed armed forces abroad at least 98 times, including the Barbary Wars, the War of 1812, the Mexican-American War and numerous other protective details and punitive expeditions around the world to protect and secure American interests and punish violations of international norms in accordance with vital national

---

[13] McDougall, *Promised Land, Crusader State,* 57.

[14] Ibid., 212.

166

interests.[15] The use of the military has expanded in the 20th and 21st centuries. However, the use of force should continue to be guided by the American System instead of the more modern traditions—Progressive Imperialism, Wilsonianism/Liberal Internationalism or Global Meliorism. The extension of the American System does not justify a militant crusade to impose an American style democratic government on another nation. These deviations simply do not represent the foreign policy tradition of the Founding Fathers or the true spirit of the American System. In fact, they are more representative of the tyranny that colonial America fought *against* in the Revolutionary War.

Expansionism

Expansionism is still part of the core foreign policy traditions, but more in the spirit than in actual territorial expansion. It represents the power to aid the larger international community through diplomacy and development. Narrowly interpreted, the United States is currently content with its present territories, which would seem to indicate that the foreign policy tradition of Expansionism is a closed chapter in American history. However, American Expansionism represented more than territorial expansion. It also represented the spread of commerce, development, community and the influence of like-minded communities that held the same common interests, values and rights throughout the continent. In fact, the expansion of American commercial relations throughout the globe championed and contributed to the expansion of globalization. The federal government also provided new lands and opportunities on the continent to expand

---

[15] Congressional Research Service, *Instances of Use of United States Armed Forces Abroad, 1798-2009, 27 January 2010.* Washington DC: Government Printing Office, 2010. 1-7.

the capabilities and resources of the nation. The frontier was opened with new infrastructure, technology, agricultural techniques and manufacturing efficiency, which aided and assisted the people in conquering and settling the expanding frontier of the continent. These forms of aid were embraced and sustained by the people. The government provided opportunities for the people to join in the "pursuit of happiness," but it was up to each individual to seize that opportunity and forge a life for themselves and their families. That is the spirit of Expansionism that needs to be infused into diplomacy and developmental aid programs.

Diplomacy and development efforts expand the *opportunities* of developing nations in accordance with their requests for assistance. Developmental aid should focus on improvements in infrastructure, technology, agricultural techniques and manufacturing efficiency to assist and encourage the people and local communities to seize opportunities and forge new lives for themselves and their families. However, the goal of developmental aid should not be used to create dependency but to create the opportunity to enable responsible independence in order to be contributing members of society. This process is slow and painful and is largely dependent on the initiative and resourcefulness of individuals, communities and nations. However, resources are limited, so development must be governed and prioritized by America's vital national interests in conjunction with the capacity and interests of international allies and partners.

The United States also expands influence by leading international organizations, treaties, alliances and coalitions, which have been designed and negotiated to facilitate an alignment of American interests, values and/or rights with international partners. These multilateral agreements and alliances represent specific communities of consent for limited purposes, such as collective defense. The "community" nature of treaties and international organizations mitigates the threat through collective action and expands American influence. For example, the North Atlantic Treaty Organization remains one of the foundational international organizations in American foreign policy. McDougall postulates that one element of international order would include "a growing web of specific treaties to which like-minded nations adhered because their sovereignty would be more secure, their power enhanced, and their interests better served inside the cooperative system than outside it."[16] This principle supports modern American Expansionism and aligns seamlessly with the true spirit of Unilateralism.

Together, these foreign policy traditions represent a synergistic combination that provide balance between national interests and national power in order to sustain civil liberty and order at home, and promote liberty and international order abroad. The goal of foreign policy in 21st century American grand strategy is to engage nations through diplomacy and development, supported by the unilateral national power to defend the nation, as well as, deter or defeat any enemy. In pursuit of this mission, sufficient means must be resourced, sustained, and balanced across the instruments of power to effectively shape and respond to the complex strategic environment with flexibility and adaptability in order to secure and promote America's vital national interests.

The traditions emphasize positive international engagement via diplomacy and development, which must be adequately resourced and balanced to remain synergistically coupled with the military power in order to check national and transnational threats and balance against competing national and international power. However, the *use* of

---

[16] McDougall, *Promised Land, Crusader State,* 218.

coercion and force must be carefully balanced with national interests and realistic strategic ends, since coercion and force are not compatible with popular sovereignty or the development of civil liberty. Ultimately, the secondary quest for international order must never compromise the national interests or the U.S. Constitution, which established and secured American civil liberty and order within the United States. Restoring these four foundational foreign policy traditions will reestablish the solid foundation of American grand strategy in the historical struggle to balance liberty and order.

CONCLUSION

The Constitution and the Declaration of Independence constitute America's first and enduring grand strategy, which continues to secure civil liberty and order for the United States. The Constitution continues to serve as an effective and *valid* grand strategy that is *suitable*, *acceptable*, and *feasible*. These founding documents remain *suitable* because they still grant sufficient power and authority to promote and secure national interests, while still effectively protecting and sustaining America's civil liberty. The Constitution is still *acceptable* because it has maintained the approval and support of both the people and the States, as amended. The Constitution remains *feasible* because the government has been granted sufficient authority and power to provide and sustain *means* to achieve the nation's strategic *ends* with flexibility and adaptability. The founding documents remain relevant and *effective* today because of the wisdom and judgment of the Founding Fathers, who based the strategic design of America's first and enduring grand strategy on the timeless lessons of history and practical experience. The critical factor that accounts for the long-term *effectiveness* of the Constitution was that the Founding Fathers accurately assessed and effectively mitigated the critical *risk* presented by the unchanging *depravity of human nature* through an innovative and sophisticated political and institutional theory, which was based on popular sovereignty.

The *effectiveness* of the U.S. Constitution to secure civil liberty and order was based on the realistic and innovative nature of American political theory, which was designed to capitalize on the lessons learned from a century and a half of experience in representative self-government in the American colonial communities. Despite the challenges of human nature, the success of America's political development was made

171

possible by the unprecedented unity of American communities driven by a core Anglo-American Protestant culture, which enabled a common set of interests, values and rights across the nation. American political theory developed directly out of these united communities, which were self-governed by representative legislatures. The Constitution is based on four major theoretical concepts that were developed from this political development, which form the core of American political theory: 1) popular sovereignty; 2) republicanism; 3) federalism; 4) extended republic; and 5) the separation of government power with checks and balances.

The central political theory of the Constitution is *popular sovereignty*, which is the concept that "the *community* and its *government* originate in the *consent* of the *people*."[1] *Popular sovereignty* created and sustained *civil liberty* through the symbiotic consensual relationship created between the people, the community, and the government, which balanced individual freedom with obedience and civil rights with civil responsibilities—see Figure 1 in Chapter 2. *Civil liberty* represented the balance *between liberty and order.* The symbiotic consensual relationship began with the people, who transferred their inherent *power*—sovereignty—to the community by *consent*. The *people* agreed it was in their *interests* to join a community and consented to restrict their *natural liberty* and accept the *civil responsibility* to obey and submit to the *majority rule* of the community based on common *values,* which formed the foundation for *civil liberty. Communities* were formed by *consent* of the *people* through a *compact*, which was a two-part agreement: 1) the individual *unanimous* agreement to form the community and submit to the *majority rule* of the collective community; and 2) a *majority* agreement

---

[1] Donald S. Lutz, *The Origins of American Constitutionalism* (Baton Rouge: Louisiana State University Press, 1988), 81.

on the type of government that will govern the community. In order to secure *civil liberty,* the community collectively instituted government by *majority consent* via a *compact* to enforce *civil order* through *laws* and *institutions* defined in a constitution in order to protect *civil rights.* Therefore, *popular sovereignty* represented the fundamental political theory in America and served as the foundational means in the Unites States for the people to transfer *power* and *sovereignty* by *consent* to the community and the government, which has sustained the *balance between liberty and order.*

Once independent of Britain, American *popular sovereignty* formally replaced the grant of power by the sovereign authority of the British Crown via *charter* with the grant of power by the sovereign authority of the people collectively in a *compact*—the Declaration of Independence. The Declaration of Independence, together with the Preamble to the Constitution, formed the national *compact* that created *a people,* established an independent nation and defined their national identity. This *compact* granted sovereign authority and power to a *federal government* designed to be both responsive and accountable to the *people*—the source of *popular sovereignty.* However, in order to provide restraints on human nature, the Constitution also defined and established the innovative institutional mechanisms of government that formalized and supported the symbiotic consensual relationship created by popular sovereignty.

The Founding Fathers developed an effective and enduring Constitution by using *institutional design to channel human nature* in order to govern effectively, as well as preserve and protect civil liberty.[2] The innovative combination of federalism, republican government, and the extended republic effectively instituted popular sovereignty in the

---

[2] Ibid., 165.

United States and prevented the tyranny of government, as well as the majority. The Constitution established a *republican* form of federal government, which instituted *popular sovereignty* by subjecting the people to laws only based on their *consent*—laws passed by the majority of elected representatives through the legislature.[3] The representative legislature collectively checked the tyranny of the majority by utilizing a deliberative process to govern the people in the long-term national interest without violating minority rights or compromising majority interests for temporary gains.[4] The Constitution also instituted a "double security" against governmental tyranny by utilizing *federalism* to balance the federal and state governments against each other, and *separation of powers*, *checks*, and *balances* to place controls within each government.[5] *Federalism* defined how the people delegated and delineated authority to state and national governments by creating the "dual citizenship" of the people as members of both sovereign states and a sovereign nation.[6] *Federalism* also preserved sufficient state sovereignty to govern an *extended republic,* which mitigated the tyranny of the majority by fracturing the natural majority into coalitions of minorities with the diverse regional and class interests associated with an expanding nation and large population.[7]

The Constitution, as America's grand strategy, provided the institutional framework to exercise popular sovereignty through a republican form of federal government in order to harness the collective wisdom and judgment of elected representatives through a deliberative process to govern the extended republic.

---

[3] Ibid., 155.

[4] Hamilton, Madison, and Jay, 76. Lutz, 85.

[5] Hamilton, Madison, and Jay, 320.

[6] Lutz, 153.

[7] Hamilton, Madison, and Jay, 321.

Ultimately, the Constitution established a government that has mitigated human nature through checks on majority and governmental tyranny in order to establish civil liberty in the United States and sustain the balance between liberty and order. Therefore, the Constitution is the foundation of an enduring and effective American grand strategy.

As America's foundational grand strategy, the Constitution established the vital *national interests* via the Preamble, which defined the *ends* and granted the authorities to the government to develop effective *ways* and *means* through a deliberative process to preserve and protect those national interests. The Constitution also granted the requisite governmental power to resource and sustain sufficient *means* to remain *flexible* and *adaptable* to effectively shape and mitigate a volatile and complex *strategic environment*. The institutional framework of the Constitution provided the power and authority to develop the *ends-ways-means* logical construct of American grand strategy to maintain civil liberty in the United States. Successive presidential administrations developed and established the specific strategic *ways* through foreign policy traditions.

The Founding Fathers designed these synergistic foreign policy traditions to integrate seamlessly with the Constitutional foundation to complete America's grand strategy. The presidential administrations led by key members of the Founding Fathers— Presidents Washington, Adams, Jefferson, Madison, and Monroe—developed the four foundational foreign policy traditions, or *ways*, that together with the Constitution guided American grand strategy for over a century. Therefore, no pithy phrase or single doctrine has ever been sufficient to express the entirety of American grand strategy. These foreign policy traditions were based on the same fundamental *assumptions* that governed the Declaration of Independence and the Constitution. The foundational assumption in the constitutional design was the *depravity of human nature*, which also demanded the sustainment of a *respectable defense posture* in order to maintain a sufficient *balance of power* to provide a *unilateral* check on international aggression in order to defend America's *civil liberty* and secure the vital national interests. America's foundational beliefs and traditions are honored by these first four traditions—American Liberty/ Exceptionalism, Unilateralism, the American System and Expansionism. This historical criticism has confirmed their effectiveness.

In conjunction with the Constitution, these foreign policy traditions seamlessly work together in an integrated system to form a holistic American grand strategy. In the pursuit of *Liberty*, America mastered self-government, declared and won independence from Britain. *American Liberty* was secured in a "more perfect Union" developed and instituted by the Founding Fathers through the Constitution. In order to maintain *Liberty*, the United States embraced *Unilateralism* to maintain a respectable defensive posture and *political neutrality* despite worldwide engagement and extensive international trade. Unilateralism was designed to insulate, not isolate, America from the imperial powers of Europe in order to preserve and protect national sovereignty. Otherwise, European politics and interests would have needlessly embroiled America in European wars contrary to national interests. In order to maintain this *Unilateralism*, an *American System* was developed and declared to protect the American continent from European imperial power and influence. In order to establish a secure *American System*, the United States pursued *Expansionism* to secure, populate, and defend the North American continent, which secured the American homeland to establish and sustain civil liberty and order free from imperial interference. These foundational foreign policy traditions developed by the Founding Fathers integrated seamlessly with the principles and assumptions of the Constitution. Therefore, these foreign policy traditions supported strategies that were realistic and effective. Since they were consistent with the Constitutional principles and effective at supporting and defending America's civil liberty, they also met the strategic logic tests of *suitability, acceptability* or *feasibility.*

In contrast, the more modern progressive traditions—Progressive Imperialism, Wilsonianism/Liberal Internationalism, and Global Meliorism—are founded on flawed strategic *assumptions* and *invalid* strategies that do not fully meet the strategic logic tests of *suitability, acceptability* or *feasibility.* However, Containment is not included in this criticism because it has proven effective and realistic as an extension of the American System, and consistent with the other foundational traditions as long as it remains *feasible.* Unlike Containment, the three progressive foreign policy traditions departed from the foundational traditions and introduced significant hidden strategic *risk* based on the following fundamentally *flawed assumptions.* The first is the assumption of the perfectibility of human nature in direct contrast with the unchanging depravity of human nature. The second is the assumption that the spread of democracies or republics will effectively prevent war to usher in a utopian state of world peace. The third assumption is that a "League" of United Nations can effectively prevent war to usher in a utopian state of world peace. The progressive theories that serve as the foundation of these modern traditions have proven to be overly idealistic and have resulted in *unrealistic ends* based on these *flawed assumptions,* which mask *strategic risks.* These flawed assumptions and unrealistic ends also drive *invalid strategies* that are inconsistent with the Constitutional principles of popular sovereignty and civil liberty, which exposed the nation to additional *strategic risk*. Ultimately, these strategic risks resulted in significant *strategic consequences*, which are demonstrated most effectively in the Philippine-American War and Vietnam War, but also, to a lesser degree, in the two more recent protracted wars in Afghanistan and Iraq. Therefore, both the lessons of history and practical experience demonstrate that these progressive foreign policy traditions have achieved limited strategic success, suffered significant strategic consequences, and violated the fundamental principles of popular sovereignty and civil liberty that undergird and empower the U.S. Constitution.

This critical analysis recommends a return to the practical wisdom and judgment of the Founding Fathers and the principles of popular sovereignty and civil liberty that undergird the U.S. Constitution. The historical analysis and criticism revealed significant strategic risks and consequences associated with the progressive traditions along with limited strategic successes secured at great sacrifice and cost. In contrast, the original traditions have proven to be successful because of the realistic assumptions and valid strategies in complete harmony with popular sovereignty and civil liberty. The practical lessons drawn from this historical criticism confirm and validate a return to America's traditional foreign policy traditions in order to reestablish American grand strategy on the solid foundation of *realistic assumptions* and *valid strategies*. **Therefore, the same enduring principles of civil liberty and order that framed America's first grand strategy through the Declaration of Independence, the U.S. Constitution and the foreign policy traditions of the Founding Fathers must frame America's Grand Strategy in the 21st century.**

Coupled seamlessly with the Constitution and updated for today's strategic environment, the four core foreign policy traditions established by the Founding Fathers—Liberty/Exceptionalism, Unilateralism, American System and Expansionism—provide a realistic full-spectrum foreign policy foundation for an effective American grand strategy for the 21st century. These foreign policy traditions represent a synergistic combination that provide balance between national sovereignty, power and interests in order to sustain civil liberty and order at home, and appropriately promote liberty and international order abroad. The traditions emphasize positive international engagement via diplomacy and development without sacrificing national sovereignty or civil liberty. However, the diplomatic and developmental means for this engagement must be adequately resourced and sustained for effectiveness. They must also be maintained in balance with military power to check national and transnational threats and balance against competing national and trans-national threats. However, the *use* of coercion and force abroad must be carefully balanced with national interests and realistic strategic ends, to ensure compatibility with popular sovereignty and the development of civil liberty. Ultimately, the secondary quest for international order must never compromise vital national interests established by the U.S. Constitution. Therefore, the goal of foreign policy in 21st century American grand strategy is to engage nations through diplomacy and development, supported by the unilateral national power to defend the nation, as well as, deter or defeat any enemy. In pursuit of this mission, sufficient means must be resourced, sustained, and balanced across the instruments of power to effectively shape and respond to a volatile and complex strategic environment with the flexibility and adaptability to promote and secure America's vital national interests.

American grand strategy will always be dependent on the collective wisdom and judgment of the President and Congress. Ultimately, the Constitution has granted them the authority and the grave responsibility to resource and sustain the best *means* available to secure America's vital national interests and *ends* in *ways* that are both acceptable and realistic. Americans count on the government to act in accordance with the Constitution and foreign policy traditions that define America's grand strategy in order to protect the Constitution and the civil liberty that defines the greatness of the United States.

The U.S. Constitution remains the foundation of American grand strategy and must be protected and never compromised. We, the people of the United States, play a critical role in protecting the most vital of America's vital interests—the Constitution itself—we must never forget the oath we have sworn our allegiance to as citizens in the service of the United States of America. "I will support and defend the Constitution of the United States against all enemies, foreign and domestic; that I will bear true faith and allegiance to the same; that I take this obligation freely, without any mental reservation or purpose of evasion; and that I will well and faithfully discharge the office upon which I am about to enter. So help me God."

BIBLIOGRAPHY

Adams, John Quincy. "An address, delivered at the request of the committee of arrangements for celebrating the Anniversary of Independence, at the city of Washington on the fourth Of July 1821 by John Quincy Adams." A Collection of Fourth of July Speeches from the Special Collections of Ellis Library, University of Missouri-Columbia. http://digital.library.umsystem.edu/cgi/t/text/text-idx?sid=508ff392ee876697f6ad60d6f09e4dc3;g=;c=jul;idno=jul000088 (accessed March 1, 2012).

------. *Memoirs of John Quincy Adams, Comprising Portions of His Diary from 1795 to 1848.* Edited by Charles Francis Adams. Philadelphia: J. B. Lippincott & Co., 1875. University of California Digital Library. http://www.archive.org/details/memjohnquinc05adamrich (accessed March 1, 2012).

------. *The Writings of John Quincy Adams,1811-1813,* vol. IV. Edited by Worthington Chauncey Ford. New York: MacMillan Company, 1914. University of California Digital Library. http://archive.org/details/fordsjohnadams04adamrich (accessed 25 May 2012).

Appleby, Joyce. *Capitalism and a New Social Order: The Republican Vision of the 1790s.* New York: New York University Press, 1984.

Armitage, Richard L. and Joseph S. Nye. *CSIS Commission on Smart Power: A Smarter, More Secure America.* Washington: Center for Strategic and International Studies, 2007.

Articles of Confederation. Avalon Project: Documents in Law, History and Diplomacy, "Articles of Confederation: March 1, 1781." Lillian Goldman Law Library, Yale Law School. http://avalon.law.yale.edu/18th_century/artconf.asp (accessed September 20, 2011).

Bayard, Samuel John. *A Sketch of the Life of Com. Robert F. Stockton.* New York: Derby and Jackson, 1856. The Library of Congress Internet Archive. http://www.archive.org/details/sketchoflifeofco00baya (Accessed March 1, 2012).

Betts, Richard K. "U.S. National Security Strategy: Lenses and Landmarks." November 2004 Paper presented for the launch conference of the Princeton Project "Toward a New National Security Strategy", May 2004. Princeton University. November 2004.

Boot, Max. *The Savage Wars of Peace: Small Wars and the Rise of American Power.* New York: Basic Books, 2003.

Bowie, Robert R. and Richard H. Immerman. *Waging Peace: How Eisenhower Shaped an Enduring Cold War Strategy*. Oxford: Oxford University Press, 1997.

Carr, Edward H. *The Twenty Years' Crisis 1919-1939: An Introduction to the Study of International Relations*. London: MacMillan & Company, 1946.

Chairman, Joint Chiefs of Staff. *National Military Strategy of the United States of America 2011: Redefining America's Military Leadership*. Washington DC: Government Printing Office, Febuary 2011.

Churchill, Winston. "The Sinews of Peace." Speech at Westminster College, Fulton, Missouri, March 5, 1946. The Churchill Centre and Museum at the Churchill War Rooms, London. https://www.winstonchurchill.org/learn/speeches/speeches-of-winston-churchill/1946-1963-elder-statesman/120-the-sinews-of-peace (accessed 25 May, 2012).

Clark, Ian. *The Post-Cold War Order: The Spoils of Peace*. Oxford: Oxford University Press, 2001.

Clausewitz, Carl Von. *On War*. Edited and Translated by Michael Howard and Peter Paret. Oxford: New York: Alfred A. Knopf, Inc., 1993.

Clemenceau, Georges. Comments on Wilson's "Peace Without Victory" Speech quoted in J. W. Schulte Nordholt, *Woodrow Wilson: A Life for World Peace*, trans. by Hebert H. Rowen (Berkeley: University of California Press, 1991), 289.

Cleveland, Henry. *Alexander H. Stephens, in Public and Private: With Letters and Speeches, Before, During, and Since the War*. Philadelphia: National Publishing Company, 1866. Hathi Trust Digital Library. http://babel.hathitrust.org/cgi/pt?view=image;size=75;id=uc1.b60934;page=root;seq=1 (Accessed 20 January 2012).

Congressional Research Service. *A Balanced Budget Constitutional Amendment: Background and Congressional Options, 8 July 2011*. Washington DC: Government Printing Office, 2011.

------. *Instances of Use of United States Armed Forces Abroad, 1798-2009, 27 January 2010*. Washington DC: Government Printing Office, 2010.

------. *The United Nations Human Rights Council: Issues for Congress, 18 July 2011*. Washington DC: Government Printing Office, 2011.

------. *United Nations Reform: U.S. Policy and International Perspectives, 7 July 2011*. Washington DC: Government Printing Office, 2011.

Croly, Herbert D. *Progressive Democracy*. New York: The Macmillan Company, 1915. American Libraries Internet Archive. http://www.archive.org/details/progressivedemo04crolgoog (Accessed 20 January 2012).

------. *The Promise of American Life*. New York: The MacMillan Company, 1911. Google Books. http://books.google.com/books/about/The_Promise_of_American_Life.html?id=3 BASAAAAYAAJ (Accessed January 20, 2012).

Drew, S. Nelson, ed. *NSC-68: Forging the Strategy of Containment*. Washington, DC: National Defense University, 1996. http://www.ou.edu/cls/online/lstd5790security/pdfs/NSC68.pdf (accessed September 12, 2011).

Fettweis, Christopher J. "Dangerous Revisionism: On the Founders, 'Neocons' and the Importance of History." *Orbis: A Journal of World Affairs*. Volume 53, Number 3, (Summer 2009): 507-523.

Fogel, Robert. "The Fourth Great Awakening and the Political Realignment of the 1990s." American Enterprise Institute for Public Policy Research, AEI Bradley Lecture Series, September 11, 1995. http://www.aei.org/speech/society-and-culture/religion/the-fourth-great-awakening-and-the-political-realignment-of-the-1990s (accessed May 25, 2012).

Flournoy, Michèle A. and Shawn W. Brimley. "Strategic Planning for National Security: A New Project Solarium." *Joint Force Quarterly*. Issue 41, (2nd Quarter 2006): 80-86.

Frohnen, Bruce, *The American Republic: Primary Sources*. Indianapolis: Liberty Fund, 2002. Chapter: "Providence Agreement August 20, 1637." http://oll.libertyfund.org/title/669/206080 (Accessed on February 2, 2012).

Fukuyama, Francis. *The End of History and the Last Man*. New York: The Free Press, 1992.

Fulbright, J. William. *The Arrogance of Power*. New York: Random House, 1967.

Galbraith, John Kenneth. "Making 'Point 4' Work: Some Unsolved Problems in Aiding Backward Areas," *Commentary* (September 1950): 229, quoted in Library of Congress, *Technical information for Congress: Report to the Subcommittee on Science, Research and Technology of the Committee on Science and Technology, U.S. House of Representatives, Ninety-sixth Congress, first session*. 3rd ed. (Washington: U.S. Government Printing Office, 1979), 95-6. Hathitrust Digital Library. http://hdl.handle.net/2027/mdp.39015081271119 (accessed May 25, 2012).

Gray, Colin S. *Hard Power and Soft Power: The Utility of Military Force as an Instrument of Policy in the 21ˢᵗ Century*. Carlisle: Strategic Studies Institute, 2011.

Hamilton, Alexander, James Madison, and John Jay. *The Federalist Papers*. Edited by Clint Rossiter. New York: New American Library, 2003.

Hart, B. H. Liddell. *Strategy*. New York: Penguin Group, 1991.

Huntington, Samuel P. *The Clash of Civilizations and the Remaking of World Order*. New York: Simon & Schuster Paperbacks, 2003.

Huntington, Samuel P. *Who Are We? The Challenges to America's National Identity*. New York: Simon & Schuster Paperbacks, 2005.

Ikenberry, G. John, and Anne Marie Slaughter. "Forging a World of Liberty Under Law: U.S. National Security in the 21ˢᵗ Century." Final Paper of the Princeton Project on National Security. Princeton University. 27 September 2006.

Iriye, Akira. *The Cambridge History of American Foreign Relations*. Vol. 3. *The Globalizing of America, 1913-1945*. Cambridge: Cambridge University Press, 1993.

Johnson, Lyndon B. *Lyndon B. Johnson: 1966 (In Two Books): Containing the Public Messages, Speeches, and Statements of the President*. Book II—July 1 to December 31, 1966. Washington: United States Government Printing Office, 1967. Hathitrust Digital Library. http://hdl.handle.net/2027/miua.4731549.1966.002 (accessed May 25, 2012).

Kant, Immanuel. *Perpetual Peace: A Philosophical Essay 1795*. Translated by M. Campbell Smith. New York: The MacMillan Company, 1917. http://files.libertyfund.org/files/357/0075_Bk.pdf (accessed 12 September, 2011)

Kennedy, Paul. *Grand Strategies in War and Peace*. New Haven: Yale University Press, 1991.

Ketcham, Ralph, ed. *The Anti-Federalist Papers and the Constitutional Convention Debates*. New York: New American Library, 2003.

Kesaris, Paul and Joan Gibson. *A Guide to Minutes and documents of the Cabinet meetings of President Eisenhower (1953-1961) [and] Minutes of telephone conversations of John Foster Dulles and of Christian Herter (1953-1961)*. Washington: University Publications of America, 1980. Microfilm.

Kesaris, Paul and Maria Schlesinger. *Minutes of Meetings of the National Security Council/First Supplement, 1953-1961.* Federick: University Publications of America, 1988. Microfilm.

Kissinger, Henry A. *American Foreign Policy.* New York: W. W. Norton & Company, Inc., 1977.

------. *Diplomacy.* New York: Simon and Schuster, 1994.

Lutz, Donald S. *The Origins of American Constitutionalism.* Baton Rouge: Louisiana State University Press, 1988.

Madison, James. "State of the Union, Fourth Annual Message, November 4, 1812." The American Presidency Project, University of California, Santa Barbara. http://www.presidency.ucsb.edu/ws/index.php?pid=29454#axzz1vvebVci6 (accessed September 20, 2011).

Mahan, A. T., Captain. *The Influence of Sea Power upon History, 1660-1783.* New York: Dover Publications, Inc., 1987.

Mayflower Compact. "Mayflower Compact: Agreement Between the Settlers at New Plymouth, 1620." Avalon Project: Documents in Law, History and Diplomacy. Lillian Goldman Law Library, Yale Law School. http://avalon.law.yale.edu/17th_century/mayflower.asp (accessed September 12, 2011).

McDougall, Walter A. *Freedom Just Around the Corner: A New American History 1585-1828.* New York: Harper Collins Publishers Inc., 2004.

------. *Promised Land, Crusader State: The American Encounter with the World Since 1776.* New York: Houghton Mifflin Company, 1997.

------. *The Constitutional History of U.S. Foreign Policy: 222 Years of Tension in the Twilight Zone.* Center for the Study of America and the West. Foreign Policy Research Institute. September 2010.

------. *Throes of Democracy.* New York: Harper Collins Publishers Inc., 2008.

Meade, Walter Russel. *Special Providence: American Foreign Policy and How It Changed the World.* New York: Alfred A. Knopf, Inc., 2001.

Millett, Allen R. and Peter Maslowski. *For the Common Defense: A Military History of the United States.* New York: The Free Press, 1984.

Monroe, James. "Monroe Doctrine: President Monroe's seventh annual message to Congress, December 2, 1823." Avalon Project: Documents in Law, History and

Diplomacy. Lillian Goldman Law Library, Yale Law School.
http://avalon.law.yale.edu/19th_century/monroe.asp (accessed September 12, 2011).

Montgomery, D. H. *The Leading Facts of American History*. Boston: Ginn & Company, 1903.

Morgenthau, Hans J. *Politics Among Nations: The Struggle for Power and Peace*. New York: Alfred A. Knopf, Inc., 1978.

Murdock, Clark A. et al. *Beyond Goldwater-Nichols: U.S. Government and Defense Reform for a New Strategic Era, Phase 2 Report*. Washington: Center for Strategic and International Studies, 2005.

Nye, Joseph S. Jr. *Soft Power: The Means to Success in World Politics*. New York: Public Affairs, 2004.

O'Sullivan, John L. "Democracy." *The United States Democratic Review* 7, Issue 27 (March 1840): 215-229, American Memory: The Nineteenth Century in Print: Periodicals, http://memory.loc.gov/cgi-bin/query/r?ammem/ncps:@field(DOCID+@lit(AGD1642-0007-18)) (accessed May 25, 2012).

Polk, James K. "James K. Polk, First Annual Message, December 2, 1845." Edited by Gerhard Peters and John Woolley. University of California at Santa Barbara, *The American Presidency Project*, http://www.presidency.ucsb.edu/ws/?pid=29486 (accessed May 25, 2012).

------. *The Diary of James K. Polk During His Presidency, 1845 to 1849*. Vol. 1. Edited by Milo Milton Quaife. Chicago: A. C. McClurg & Co., 1910. HathiTrust Digital Library, http://hdl.handle.net/2027/loc.ark:/13960/t6d221j44?urlappend=%3Bseq=117 (accessed May 25, 2012).

Pratt, Julius W. "The Origin of 'Manifest Destiny.'" *The American Historical Review* 32, no. 4 (July 1927): 795-798. http://www.jstor.org/stable/1837859 (accessed 25 May 2012).

Record, Jeffrey. *Making War, Thinking History: Munich, Vietnam, and Presidential Uses of Force from Korea to Kosovo*. Annapolis: Naval Institute Press, 2002.

Roosevelt, Theodore. "Transcript of Theodore Roosevelt's Corollary to the Monroe Doctrine (1905)." Our Documents: 100 Milestone Documents from the National Archives. http://ourdocuments.gov/doc.php?flash=true&doc=56&page=transcript (accessed September, 12, 2011).

Saxe, John Godfrey. *The Poems of John Godfrey Saxe.* Boston: Ticknor and Fields, 1868.

Secretary of Defense. *Quadrennial Defense Review.* Washington DC: Government Printing Office, Febuary 2011.

Secretary of Homeland Security. *Quadrennial Homeland Security Review Report: A Strategic Framework for a Secure Homeland.* Washington DC: Government Printing Office, Febuary 2010.

Secretary of State. *Leading Through Civilian Power: The First Quadrennial Diplomacy and Development Review.* Washington DC: Government Printing Office, Febuary 2010.

Nordholt, J. W. Schulte. *Woodrow Wilson: A Life for World Peace.* Translated by Hebert H. Rowen. Berkeley: University of California Press, 1991.

Smith, Adam. *The Wealth of Nations.* Edited by Edwin Cannan. New York: Bantam Dell, 2003.

Smith, Timothy. "Righteousness and Hope: Christian Holiness and the Millennial Vision in America, 1880-1900." American Quarterly 31, no. 1 (Spring 1979): 21-45. http://www.jstor.org/discover/10.2307/2712485?uid=3739936&uid=2129&uid=2&uid=70&uid=4&uid=3739256&sid=47699037800717 (accessed May 25, 2012).

Strong, Josiah. *Our Country: Its Possible Future and Its Present Crisis.* New York: The Baker & Taylor Co., 1885. Internet Archive: American Libraries. http://www.archive.org/details/ourcountryitspo07strogoog (accessed March 1, 2012).

Summers, Harry G., Jr. *On Strategy: A Critical Analysis of the Vietnam War.* New York: Dell, 1984.

Tocqueville, Alexis De. *Democracy in America.* Translated by Gerald E. Bevan. London: Penguin Books Ltd., 1971.

Truman, Harry S. "Truman Doctrine: President Harry S. Truman's Address Before a Joint Session of Congress, March 12, 1947." Avalon Project: Documents in Law, History and Diplomacy. Lillian Goldman Law Library, Yale Law School. http://avalon.law.yale.edu/20th_century/trudoc.asp (accessed September 20, 2011).

Tzu, Sun. *The Art of War.* Translated by Samuel B. Griffith. New York: Oxford University Press, 1971.

United Nations. *The Universal Declaration of Human Rights.* General Assembly
Resolution 217A (III), 10 December 1948. Paris, 1948.

U.S. Code. Title 42, Chapter 122, "Native Hawaiian Health Care," Section 11701.
Findings, 01/03/2012 (112-90), The Office of the Law Revision Counsel.
http://uscode.house.gov/download/pls/42C122.txt (accessed 25 May, 2012).

U.S. Joint Chiefs of Staff. *Doctrine for the Armed Forces of the United States.* Joint
Publication 1. Washington DC: Joint Chiefs of Staff, May 02, 2007, Incorporating
Change 1, March 20, 2009.

U.S. National Security Council. *A Report to the National Security Council: NSC
Memorandum 162/2*, 30 October 1953.
http://www.fas.org/irp/offdocs/nsc-hst/nsc-162-2.pdf (accessed September 12,
2011).

U.S. President. The White House. *National Security Action Memorandum No. 52 (NSAM
52)*. John F. Kennedy Presential Library and Museum. National Security Action
Memoranda. Document images from the Presidential Papers of John Fitzgerald
Kennedy, National Security Files. http://www.jfklibrary.org/Asset-
Viewer/KDit5FSwHEmiuwttNVhDZQ.aspx (accessed March 1, 2012).

------. *National Security Strategy.* Washington DC: Government Printing Office,
September 2002.

------. *National Security Strategy.* Washington DC: Government Printing Office, March
2006.

------. *National Security Strategy.* Washington DC: Government Printing Office, May
2010.

Vandenberg, Arthur H., "American Foreign Policy, January 10, 1945." *Congressional
Record*, 79th Congress, 1st Session, 164-67, United States Senate, Senate.gov,
http://www.senate.gov/artandhistory/history/resources/pdf/VandenbergSpeech.pdf
(accessed 25 May, 2012).

Washington, George. "George Washington's Farewell Address, 1796." Avalon Project:
Documents in Law, History and Diplomacy. Lillian Goldman Law Library, Yale
Law School. http://avalon.law.yale.edu/18th_century/washing.asp (accessed
September 20, 2011).

------. *The Writings of George Washington from the original Manuscript Sources, 1745-
1799.* Edited by John C. Fitzpatrick. Washington: United States Printing Office,
1931-44. University of Virginia Library electronic text.
http://etext.virginia.edu/washington/fitzpatrick/ (accessed February 29, 2012).

Watterson, Henry. *History of the Spanish-American War; Embracing A Complete Review of Our Relations with Spain.* San Francisco: E. D. Bronson & Co., 1898. Internet Archive, University of California, California Digital Library. http://archive.org/stream/spanishamwar00wattrich (accessed May 25, 2012).

Wilkes, Charles. *United States' Exploring Expedition, During the Years 1838-1842.* London: Whittaker and Co., 1845. HathiTrust Digital Library. http://hdl.handle.net/2027/uc2.ark:/13960/t59c6th8j (accessed May 25, 2012).

Wilson, Woodrow. "8 January, 1918: President Woodrow Wilson's Fourteen Points." Avalon Project: Documents in Law, History and Diplomacy. Lillian Goldman Law Library, Yale Law School. http://avalon.law.yale.edu/20th_century/wilson14.asp (accessed September 20, 2011).

------. *Congressional Government: A Study in American Politics.* 15th Edition. Boston: Houghton Mifflin Company, 1900. http://books.google.com/books/about/Congressional_government.html?id=Xx5E AQAAIAAJ (Accessed January 20, 2012).

Yarger, Harry R. "Strategic Theory for the 21st Century: The Little Book on Big Strategy." Strategic Studies Institute (SSI) monograph, February 2006. http://www.comw.org/qdr/fulltext/0602yarger.pdf (accessed September 12, 2011).

VITA

Col Daniel L. Waters (USAF)

Col Daniel L. Waters most recently served as Deputy Group Commander, 58th Operations Group, 58th Special Operations Wing at Kirtland AFB, New Mexico. He was commissioned in 1990. Following initial training, he served as the Chief of Air Terminal Operations Center at Pope AFB, followed by several flying tours in the C-130E and HC-130P with multiple combat tours in Bosnia and Afghanistan. He served as the Chief, Joint Training Systems in the USSOCOM J7 with a follow on assignment as Commander, Detachment 1 (MV-22 Training), 58th Operations Group at New River Marine Corps Air Station, North Carolina. He then served as Commander, 58th Training Squadron at Kirtland Air Force Base. Col Waters is a graduate of the U.S. Air Force Academy with a Bachelors Degree in Economics, as well as, a graduate of Air University with a Masters Degree in Military Operational Art and Science.

www.ingramcontent.com/pod-product-compliance
Lightning Source LLC
Chambersburg PA
CBHW081324310526
45789CB00018B/2337